"Another book by Chester and Timmis that is full of biblical insight and much practical wisdom for daily, street-level ministry in our Western culture today."

Tim Keller, Senior Pastor, Redeemer Presbyterian Church, New York City; best-selling author, *The Reason for God*

"I was deeply convicted and excited after reading *Total Church,* so it was great to see the principles of that book further developed in *Everyday Church.* Because these principles are so clearly biblical, they are therefore not optional—which means we must all find ways to live out these truths if the church is to be the radiant bride she was meant to be. I look forward to the new joy that believers will experience as they pursue church as described in this book."

Francis Chan, author, *Crazy Love*

"Chester and Timmis have once again challenged us to think differently and diligently about gospel-centered community and gospel-centered mission. In so doing they have given us some answers of how to engage the growing chasm between the church and world with faithfulness to the gospel."

Matt Chandler, Lead Pastor, The Village Church, Highland Village, Texas; author, *The Explicit Gospel*

"There are few whom God uses to rattle my bones about true gospel focus, few who can help me to organize and declutter the simple and sacrificial applications of the cross, like Tim Chester and Steve Timmis. God has raised them up to help us to see the work of the church through a lens of soul conformity. God uses them to give us clear sight of why the church exists and what our gospel-empowered focus should resemble. Any church of any size and any location can hit the ground running with the biblically rich and accessible truths that resound from *Everyday Church.*"

Eric Mason, Lead Pastor, Epiphany Fellowship, Philadelphia, Pennsylvania

"Chester and Timmis remind us that Christianity is n   er of Western culture; it has drifted to the margins I found myself inspired and hopeful while r Christianity began on the margins yet   its world. If you're tired of the 'same old, s   urch, and you long for something that pierces and   then *Everyday Church* is for you."

Bryan Loritts, Lead Pastor, Fellowship M   , Memphis, Tennessee

EVERYDAY CHURCH

EVERYDAY CHURCH

GOSPEL COMMUNITIES ON MISSION

TIM CHESTER & STEVE TIMMIS

CROSSWAY

WHEATON, ILLINOIS

Everyday Church: Gospel Communities on Mission

Copyright © 2012 by Tim Chester and Steve Timmis

North American edition published by Crossway

Published by Crossway
        1300 Crescent Street
        Wheaton, Illinois 60187

Originally published by Inter-Varsity Press, Nottingham, England. Copyright 2011 by Tim Chester and Steve Timmis. North American edition publishing by permission of Inter-Varsity.

Cover design and image: Matt Naylor

Art direction: Patrick Mahoney, The Mahoney Design Team

First printing 2012

Printed in the United States of America

ISBN-13: 978-1-4335-3222-1
ISBN-10: 1-4335-3222-0
ePub ISBN: 978-1-4335-4264-0
PDF ISBN: 978-1-4335-4262-6
Mobipocket ISBN: 978-1-4335-4263-3

Library of Congress Cataloging-in-Publication Data

Chester, Tim.
   Everyday church: Gospel communications on mission /
Tim Chester and Steve Timmis.—North American ed.
      p. cm.
   Includes bibliographical references and index.
   ISBN 978-1-4335-3222-1 (tp)
   1. Bible. N.T. Peter, 1st—Commentaries. I. Timmis,
Steve, 1957-   II. Title.
BS2795.53.C44   2012
227'.9207—dc23   2012006166

Crossway is a publishing ministry of Good News Publishers.

VP		24	23	22	21	20	19	18	17	16	15
16	15	14	13	12	11	10	9	8	7	6	5	4

CONTENTS

INTRODUCTION

In 1915 Tim's grandmother moved to a two-up, two-down terraced house in Darlington, an industrial town in the north of England. She was one year old. The street was still being built when she moved. So was the Methodist chapel two streets over. That house became her home for the next ninety years, and the chapel became a second home.

When my mother was a child, the congregation was comprised of one hundred attendees, with a choir of twenty plus another fifty children in the Sunday school. More than that, the church was at the heart of neighborhood life. Church concerts, church teas, church outings—these were the only alternatives to the pub that most working-class people in the area had. My grandmother and my mother grew up with the church at the center of their lives. My grandmother was still playing the piano on Sunday mornings into her nineties. Her failing hearing meant she had trouble hearing the singing, but there was no one else.

Today, the congregation has dwindled to just a dozen or so people, none of whom are under fifty. Local people have other things to do on a Sunday morning. Choir recitals cannot compete with the Xbox and *The X Factor*. The building, freshly constructed when my grandmother began attending, has become a relic, a monument to a former way of life. It plays no part in the lives of all but a handful of people. It is part of the neighborhood's history but not its present.

Christians today increasingly find themselves on the margins of the culture. We live in a post-Christian culture. The majority of people in the West today have no intention of ever attending church.

Most name the name of Christ only as a swearword. Some prominent churches are growing, but much of this is transfer growth rather than true evangelistic growth.

However, many of our approaches to evangelism still assume a Christendom mentality. We expect people to come when we ring the church bell or put on a good service, but the majority of the population are disconnected from church. Changing what we do in church will not reach them. We need to meet them in the context of everyday life. Our previous book, *Total Church*, argued that the Christian gospel and the Christian community should be central to every aspect of our life and mission.[1] This book builds on that foundation. It is a call for us to be *an everyday church with an everyday mission*. We need to shift our focus from putting on attractional events to creating attractional communities. Our marginal status is an opportunity to rediscover the missionary call of the people of God. We can recover witness to Christ unmuddied by nominal Christianity.

It is also an opportunity to reconnect with our Bibles. The New Testament is a collection of missionary documents written to missionary situations. It was written by Christians living on the margins of their culture. Throughout this book we want to enter into a dialogue with the first letter of Peter. Peter was writing to Christians who found themselves "strangers and exiles" in the first-century Roman Empire. They were on the margins facing slander and abuse, much as we are. This is not a commentary. Instead we offer some missional reflections on 1 Peter to explore what the Spirit would say to the Western church today through this portion of God's Word. Above all, we have tried to write a practical book that shows what everyday church and everyday mission might look like on the ground.

In calling the church to everyday mission we recognize that this is what many Christians are already doing: being good neighbors, colleagues, and family members; doing good in the face of hostility; and bearing witness to Christ in the context of ordinary life. Our aim is not to dismiss this. Quite the opposite. We want to celebrate it and put it back at the center of the church's mission, and perhaps also give it more direction and show how it can be more intentional.

We have written this book together and so generally use plural pronouns (we, us). But where we describe an experience or story particular to one of us, we have used a singular pronoun (I, me).

1

LIFE AT THE MARGINS

1 PETER 1:1–12

It is easy for Christians to feel discouraged when we read about declining church attendance or see the growing secularization of our culture, but we are excited about the future. In many ways the opposite of secularism is actually nominalism, so growing secularism is an opportunity to develop witness to Christ unclouded by nominal faith. Much of the decline in the church in the West has been the falling off of nominal Christians. As a result, what remains may be more healthy. We have the opportunity to become communities focused on Jesus and his mission. The number of true Christians may not be falling so steeply—if at all. What is fast disappearing is the opportunity to reach notionally religious people through church activities.

To seize these new opportunities, we first need to recognize that the Christian gospel has moved from the center of our culture to the margins.

LIVING IN A POST-CHRISTIAN CONTEXT

One hundred million people in the United States have no contact with church.[1] Among this group are an estimated thirteen to fifteen million people who express a commitment to Christ and accept him as their Savior. This still leaves *eighty-five million Americans who are unchurched and unbelieving.*

The Easter 2009 edition of *Newsweek* magazine created a stir with the words "The Decline and Fall of Christian America" embla-zoned across its front cover.[2] The cover article by Jon Meacham quotes Al Mohler saying, "Clearly, there is a new narrative, a post-Christian narrative, that is animating large portions of this society." The num-ber of adults in the United States who do not attend church has nearly doubled since 1991. Over 3,500 United States churches close their doors every year, and the attendance of more than 80 percent of those remaining has plateaued or is declining.[3] Researcher Mike Regele con-cludes: "The combined impact of the Information Age, postmodern thought, globalization, and racial-ethnic pluralism that has seen the demise of the grand American story also has displaced the historic role the church has played in that story. As a result, we are seeing the marginalization of the institutional church."[4]

Since the Enlightenment, Western intellectuals have assumed a link between modernity and secularization. Some rejoiced in this "progress" while others lamented the reduction of everything to "rationality," but they shared the assumption that modern societies would become secular societies. This secularization theory has been challenged by sociologist Peter Berger. "Not to put too fine a point on it," he says, but "they were mistaken. Modernity is *not* intrinsically secularizing, though it has been so in particular cases."[5] The modern world is not becoming more secular. If anything it is becoming more religious.

But Berger identifies two exceptions. The first is geographic: Western and Central Europe. The second is sociological: the elites of the Western world. Pointing to a survey that named India as the world's most religious country and Sweden as the world's most secular country, Berger quips that the United States is a nation of Indians ruled over by Swedes. In other words, it is a highly religious nation, but its elites are deeply secular, even antireligious. So America *feels* more secular than it actually is. This has been the experience of Americans coming to do mission in the United Kingdom. They thought of the United States as a secular context until they came to Europe and encountered secular attitudes not only in the media but also among most ordinary people.

Although he refutes secularization theory, Berger does believe modernity changes the position of the church in the culture. "Modernity is not necessarily secularizing; it is necessarily *pluralizing*. Modernity is characterized by an increasing plurality, within the same society, of different beliefs, values, and worldviews. Plurality does indeed pose a challenge to all religious traditions—each one must cope with the fact that there are 'all these others,' not just in a faraway country but right next door."[6]

Pluralism means that although mainstream America is not secular, it is not necessarily Christian. We should not mistake religiosity for biblical faith. In the eighteenth century, American Christianity was the dominant worldview. Not any more. Now Western societies are a melting pot of worldviews. We can no longer assume that if people want to find God or discover meaning or cope with a personal crisis, they will go to church. They may attend any number of religious bodies or sects. Or they may go to a therapist. Or read a self-help book. Merely opening our doors each Sunday is no longer sufficient. Offering a good product is not enough.

It may be that middle America follows the lead of its cities and becomes more secular. Or it may be that America becomes an increasingly divided nation with secular elites but with a religious heartland. What is clear is that great swathes of America will not be reached through Sunday morning services.

What is true of the United States is even more true of Europe. America remains a far more Christianized culture than that of Europe. Research by the Barna Group in 2008 found that only one in four adults in the United States had no contact with the church, while 62 percent had attended church in the past month and a further 15 percent had had some contact over the past year.[7]

An American friend who has worked in Europe for the last seven years revisited the United States recently. As he sat drinking coffee in a MacDonald's in Florida, he was shocked to overhear so many people talking about Jesus or church as they waited in line to order. This doesn't happen in Europe! While one in four Americans has no contact with church, in Britain it is three in four.[8] Even in the supposedly more secular areas of the United States, the Northwest and Northeast, the unchurched are still a minority.[9] Moreover, among unchurched Americans there is a high level of sympathy for Christianity and even confessions of faith in Christ. Among those not attending church, 59 percent consider themselves to be Christian and 17 percent express a commitment to Christ and believe they will experience heaven after death through their acceptance of Christ as their Savior. Additionally, 19 percent of those not attending church read the Bible during a typical week, and 62 percent pray.[10] In comparison only one in four people in the United Kingdom believes in a personal God who hears prayer.

When my wife and I (Tim) first moved into our current home in England, we got talking with our new neighbor, an elderly woman who lives alone. During the conversation we told her we had moved to the area to be part of a new church. "I'm glad you're Christians," she told us, before adding that she too was a Christian. It turns out, however, that she never attends church, and she has resisted all our attempts to talk to her about Jesus. So what did she mean when she said she was a Christian? Perhaps she meant that she is a nice person and good neighbor (which she is). Perhaps she meant she is not a Muslim (her neighbors on the other side are a Muslim family originating from Pakistan, as are perhaps a third of the people living on our road). What is clear is that she did not mean she is a Christian by any biblical definition of the word. To her, "Christian" is a cultural or ethnic label. It is not a declaration of her faith in Jesus as her Savior, or her allegiance to him as her Lord, or her membership of his redeemed people.

I think of my neighbor when I hear that, according to a 2001 United Kingdom government census, 72 percent of the United Kingdom population claim to be Christian. From this we might suppose that the United Kingdom is a Christian country with little need for church planting, but figures for church attendance reveal a very different picture. In 1851 around one in four people in the United Kingdom was a churchgoer. Now it is one in ten,[11] though only about half of these are actually in church on any given Sunday.[12] Of these, 40 percent go to evangelical churches.[13] If present trends continue, average weekly church attendance in England will fall to 4.1 percent in 2020—one in twenty-five.[14]

Philip Richter and Leslie Francis categorize people as "churched" (regular or fringe churchgoers), "de-churched" (people who have been regular or fringe churchgoers at some point in the past but are so no longer) and "nonchurched" or "unchurched" (people who have had no significant contact with the church at any point).[15] Based on their findings, the *Mission-Shaped Church* report concluded that the United Kingdom population is 20 percent churched, 40 percent de-churched, and 40 percent nonchurched.[16] A 2007 Tearfund report found that almost 70 percent of the United Kingdom population has no intention of attending a church service at any point in the future.[17] And this figure is set to increase over the coming years with affiliation to Christianity and attendance at church lower among young people. Only a third of sixteen- to thirty-four-year-olds call themselves Christians.

Seventy percent of the United Kingdom population have no intention of ever attending a church service. That means new styles of worship will not reach them. That means fresh expressions of church will not reach them. That means Alpha and Christianity Explored evangelistic courses will not reach them. That means guest services will not reach them. That means churches meeting in pubs will not reach them. That means toddler churches meeting at the end of the school day will not reach them. The vast majority of unchurched and de-churched people would not turn to the church even if faced with difficult personal circumstances or in the event of national tragedies.[18] It is not a question of "improving the product" of church meetings and evangelistic events. It means reaching people apart from meetings and events.

Despite the fall in overall church attendance, only one in six regular churchgoers thinks the church he or she attends is declining in numbers. Two-fifths think their church is growing.[19] Perhaps some people are in denial about falling church numbers. But it may also be that many churches are growing but mainly through transfer growth. A declining number of Christians are consolidating into growing churches. It is still possible to grow a church by offering a better church experience than other churches. Whatever the merits of this, it is vital for us to realize that this is not evangelistic growth. It is possible to plant a church and see it grow *without doing mission.* "People can be attracted to a church by what it offers," says Jim Petersen, "but . . . increase of this sort isn't church growth at all. It's just a reshuffling of the same fifty-two cards."[20]

In the rest of Europe church attendance is higher than in the United Kingdom in Catholic and Orthodox countries, but across Europe Christian faith is at best nominal. The ten "mega-peoples" least responsive to the gospel are all found in Europe, according to the World Christian Database.[21] A report by Greater Europe Mission concludes: "Although Europe has a high percentage of people who consider themselves Christians, the data shows that Europe has the least population percentage of Christians who consider themselves committed and evangelical."[22] Europe is the world's most secular continent.

In Australia 68 percent of people may claim to be Christian, but like the United Kingdom this is largely nominal. Church attendance was 8 percent in 2001, down from 35 percent in 1966.[23] As in the United Kingdom, it is the younger generation that is missing from the Australian church.[24] A church planter in Perth wrote recently, "Many of my work colleagues are very suspicious of, or hostile, to Christianity. . . . I think in my work context in Perth it must be 'easier' to be openly and proudly gay than openly and proudly Christian."[25]

Two observations are pertinent. First, we cannot assume models of church growth from the United States will work in Europe. There is much that we can learn from the practice and theology of the American church. Our own experience in The Crowded House is testimony to that. But we cannot automatically import church growth and church planting models. In the United States you can still plant a church by creating a better church experience. If you do this in the United Kingdom, then the best you can do is attract existing churchgoers. That might be a valid endeavor, but *it is not evangelistic growth.*

Second, parts of the United States are heading in the direction of

Europe. It may be time for the United States church to learn from the European church's experience of being on the margins of the culture. George G. Hunter concludes, "As measured by the simple indicator of church attendance, nations that were once substantially Christian are now largely lost to the Christian movement."[26]

LIVING IN A POST-CHRISTENDOM CONTEXT

We are living not only in a post-Christian context but in a post-Christendom context. Christendom is the formal or informal alliance of church and state that was the dominant model in Europe from the conversion of Constantine in the fourth century AD onward. The state authorized the church while the church supported the state. Christianity became a civil religion. To be born into the states of Europe was to be born into the church. The church as an institution was given special privileges. This mutual legitimization was symbolized in the overtly Christian coronation oaths, parliamentary prayers and sermons, the parish system, the coronation of monarchs by archbishops, and so on. The United States formerly separated church and state and allowed for religious toleration, but in other ways Christendom has been as strong in the United States as in Europe. The assumption is that Christianity should have a privileged status in the cultural and political discourse of the nation. Presidents and would-be presidents overtly reference their faith and close their speeches with the words, "God bless America."

Christendom, however, is increasingly a spent force in the West. Some of the symbolism remains. The British monarch is still the head of an established church, and bishops still sit in the upper chamber of the United Kingdom Parliament. But the reality of Christendom is fading fast, overtaken by secularism and pluralism. The Bible no longer has authority in public discourse. The church no longer has a privileged voice. Church leaders still get invited to state occasions, but on matters of ethics they are ignored. When the Pope visited the United Kingdom in 2010 he was greeted with all due pomp and ceremony as a head of state. But when it comes to his views on abortion and homosexuality, he is ignored by politicians and ridiculed by the media. Lyndon Bowring, the Executive Chairman of CARE, said in an interview, "The greatest challenge . . . is the growing secularization of society, where Christianity is being increasingly squeezed out of our national life. The ultimate result of this tendency will be a society that is hostile to Christian truth and practice."[27]

In his book *After Christendom* Stuart Murray defines *post-Christendom* as "the culture that emerges as the Christian faith loses coherence within a society that has been definitively shaped by the Christian story and as the institutions that have been developed to express Christian convictions decline in influence." He also identifies seven transitions that mark the shift from Christendom to a post-Christendom culture:

1) *From the center to margins.* In Christendom the Christian story and the churches were central, but in post-Christendom these are marginal.
2) *From majority to minority.* In Christendom Christians comprised the (often overwhelming) majority, but in post-Christendom we are a minority.
3) *From settlers to sojourners.* In Christendom Christians felt at home in a culture shaped by their story, but in post-Christendom we are aliens, exiles, and pilgrims in a culture where we no longer feel at home.
4) *From privilege to plurality.* In Christendom Christians enjoyed many privileges, but in post-Christendom we are one community among many in a plural society.
5) *From control to witness.* In Christendom churches could exert control over society, but in post-Christendom we exercise influence only through witnessing to our story and its implications.
6) *From maintenance to mission.* In Christendom the emphasis was on maintaining a supposedly Christian status quo, but in post-Christendom it is on mission within a contested environment.
7) *From institution to movement.* In Christendom churches operated mainly in institutional mode, but in post-Christendom we must become again a Christian movement.[28]

The legacy of Christendom is hotly debated. Some Christians recognize that it has come to an end but believe it leaves a largely positive legacy. Others celebrate its passing, bemoaning the compromises it imposed on the church. The church's privileged status in society, they believe, meant it had a vested interest in the status quo, which inevitably blunted its proclamation of the social dimensions of repentance and meant the church was aligned, or was perceived to be aligned, with the establishment.

The future of Christendom is also debated. Historian Philip Jenkins predicts a growing non-Western Christendom doing battle with militant Islam across the so-called Third World.[29] Our focus, however, is on the West.

Here some Christians want to hang on to the last vestiges of Christendom, or they talk up the statistics of Christian affiliation however notional. Lynda Barley, head of research and statistics for the Church of England, claims, for example, that "Britain is still a predominantly Christian country," because, when asked in the census about their religion, more than seven in ten people consider themselves to be Christian.[30] Yet a 2007 poll found that only 22 percent of men and 26 percent of women in Britain agreed with the statement, "I believe in a personal god who created the world and hears my prayers."[31] So by any definition of Christian faith, almost two-thirds of those who say they are Christians clearly are not, for they do not even believe in a personal God.[32] So why claim that the West is still predominately Christian? Because some Christians want to retain the notion that Western nations are Christian with the privileges and securities this brings. It allows us to continue on the basis of business as usual.

The *Mission-Shaped Church* report is more realistic: "The Christian story is no longer at the heart of the nation. Although people may identify themselves as 'Christian' in the national census, for the majority that does not involve belonging to a worshipping community, or any inclination that it should. Many people have no identifiable religious interest or expression."[33]

We are not pessimistic. There are many signs of life. Many churches are healthy. We sense a growing commitment to church planting across all the different tribes of evangelicalism. God's Word is still being proclaimed. The gospel is still the power of God for salvation.

The Lord's arm is not too short that it cannot save. The Holy Spirit is alive and well in the world today. Christ will build his church. Our aim in reviewing these statistics is not to make us give up. Our aim is to show that the ways we do mission have to change.

CHRISTENDOM EVANGELISM IN A POST-CHRISTENDOM CULTURE

I, Steve, got into church planting in a strange way. In order to marry the woman of my dreams, I sat in the front room of her parents' house, asking her father for her hand in marriage. Her mother intervened: I could marry their daughter if I had a job and a house. It was Easter, and I was graduating in June with prospects of neither job nor house. Their daughter, waiting anxiously outside the room, was horrified to hear this stipulation. My girlfriend was even more horrified when she heard me agree. I left the house and cycled five miles in the dark to a man in a small village whom I knew had an empty building and a desire to start a church. I was twenty-two years old, but in two weeks I had a position and with it the house and job (supplemented by milking cows). We were able to get married within a few months.

On my first day in the job I started knocking on doors in the village. Every door was opened and then closed again. The same happened on the second day. And the third. So on the fourth day I got myself a clerical dog collar. From then on the doors were opened and I was warmly received. Being seen as a clergyman still had currency. Respect was still shown to the church. That was thirty years ago. Those days are now long gone.

There is nothing particularly new in our analysis of the demise of Christendom. But most of the attention in the discussion on the future of Christendom has focused on the impact of its demise on the church's involvement in the wider culture and politics. Few have addressed what it means for the local church.

For all its vital rediscovery of gospel-centered theology, the Reformation in Europe did not lead to a recovery of gospel-centered mission by local churches. That is because the Reformers generally accepted the Christendom presupposition that Europe was Christian. To be born was to be born into the church. So the church's mission to the surrounding society was pastoral rather than evangelistic. Later, with the rise of the evangelical movement, evangelism returned, in the words of Stuart Murray, "as a response to the rather belated recognition that Europe was, at best, only nominally Christian." Murray adds:

> But evangelism was still operating within a Christendom framework. Within Europe, it was assumed that the Christian story and the main tenets of the Christian message were familiar, so evangelism primarily involved repeated attempts to re-energise faith and commitment that seemed lukewarm. The emphasis was on calling people to make a renewed commitment to the implications of the gospel and to express this by activities such as reading the Bible, attending church more regularly, living morally respectable lives, and meeting the needs of others in a society without a welfare state. Beyond Europe, despite the heroic and often exemplary efforts of dedicated pioneer missionaries, evangelism too often degenerated into attempts to coerce or induce conversion and to impose a supposedly Christian and superior European culture on other societies.[34]

As a student Tim belonged to a lively, evangelistic church. Each Sunday evening someone was interviewed at the front and asked how he or she had become a Christian. Week after week the same phrase kept cropping up: "My faith came alive." Most stories were of people who had attended church as a child, but only when they came to university did their "faith come alive." Evangelistic fruit came from, as Murray puts it, "attempts to re-energise faith." And fruit there truly was. Nominal Christians were becoming living Christians. It was joy to hear those stories each week. But the opportunities to reenergize faith are diminishing fast as our culture becomes post-Christian.

We want to suggest that most of our current dominant models of church and evangelism are Christendom models. This needs to change as we move to a post-Christendom and post-Christian context.

Because we regard people as innately Christian in orientation, we think we can reach them through church meetings. So we invite people to our Sunday services or traditional celebrations in the church calendar (such as Christmas, Easter, and Thanksgiving) or special guest services or evangelistic courses. We've often been asked how we do mission without a notice board or public front door; people ask, "What about people who want to wander in off the streets?" The assumption is that mission equals a public presence.

We ring the church bell and expect people to come to our meetings to hear the gospel.

We also build evangelism around the traditional rites of passage. We connect with people through christenings, marriages, and funerals. We use baptism and marriage classes to present the gospel. We use these occasions to invite people to attend church regularly. To put it more colloquially, we reach people through the opportunities presented by "hatch, match, and dispatch."

A Christendom model seeks to exploit our perceived privileged status on Main Street. We assume a dog collar will still open doors. We assume clergymen will have a position of standing in society. We assume that events advertised on our notice board will draw people into the building. We assume we have a right to be heard when this is no longer the case and means we are perceived as strident and self-interested.

There is nothing wrong with any of these endeavors and a lot that is right with them, but they are fading opportunities. The number of christenings, church funerals, and church weddings is falling, as is attendance at Christian festivals.[35]

> The Church of England bases a significant part of its identity on its physical presence in every community, and on a "come to us" strategy. But as community becomes more complex, mere geographical presence is no longer a guarantee that we can connect. The reality is that mainstream culture no longer brings people to the church door. We can no longer assume that we can automatically reproduce ourselves, because the pool of people who regard church as relevant or important is decreasing with every generation.[36]

John Finney's research *Finding Faith Today* showed that "the most important evangelistic work of the minister appears to be not in the church and the pulpit but in two other kinds of relationships: one to one meetings with non-Christians and the 'lapsed' [and] group situations, particularly those where there is an opportunity to talk about the nature of faith."[37] His survey of recent converts found that only 4 percent said evangelistic events were the main factor with a further 13 percent saying they were a supporting factor.

There are three hundred thousand Mirpuri people in the United Kingdom from the Azad Kashmir region of Pakistan. There is no Mirpuri church. This is one of the largest unreached people groups in the world, and they are on our doorstep. So why is the United Kingdom church not throwing resources into evangelism among Mirpuris? No doubt there are many reasons. But perhaps one is the assumption that they are not our mission field. Some people, imbibing the spirit of the age, question whether we should evangelize people of other religions. Evangelicals may not think this, but perhaps unconsciously we assume we are called to reach people we somehow regard as dormant Christians. Stuart Murray says, "Arguing we should not evangelise other faith communities implies that we should evangelise only 'latent Christians' and that evangelism is unpleasant—both concepts deeply rooted in Christendom thinking."[38]

A newer feature of a Christendom approach is the outsourcing to "faith communities" of government services. Christian involvement in social action has a long and honorable tradition,[39] but more recently faith communities are being paid by governments to provide charitable services. This is promoted both by the church and by a government state eager to reduce the size of the state. The danger is that this becomes a new way in which the church becomes an arm of the state. Along the way, its dependence on state funding with its attendant requirements may blunt the church's prophetic role and evangelistic proclamation. This is not an argument against the practice, but it is a call for us to be alert to its inherent dangers.

REACHING THE EIGHTY-FIVE MILLION

As we have seen, approximately eighty-five million people in the United States have no intention of attending a church service. In the United Kingdom it is forty million—70 percent of the population.

That of course means there are still many people who attend church meetings occasionally or are open to doing so in the future. So the Christendom models still have plenty of mileage in them. We are not suggesting that churches shut down evangelistic courses, guest services, Sunday schools, and so on. Many churches will see gospel fruit from such activities for years to come. We praise God for these opportunities and rejoice when churches work effectively to reach such people. But how will we reach the eighty-five million? Or the forty million? These are the critical questions, because these numbers are only going to increase.

Anecdotally church leaders recognize that we are largely reaching people on the fringe or the openly dechurched. People are "returning" to church. Research by John Finney in the 1990s showed three-quarters of those coming to faith in the United Kingdom were from dechurched backgrounds.[40] But the number of people in the future who will return to church is dwindling all the time.

Consider attendance at Sunday school. In the United Kingdom in 1900 it was 55 percent. By 1940 it was 35 percent. By 1970 it had dropped to 14 percent. In 2000 it was just 4 percent. If the current trend continues, this will drop to only one in one hundred by 2016. One in seven forty-year-olds went to Sunday school, which means only one in seven forty-year-olds might return to church. In the future the number of potential returnees will dwindle to one in twenty and then one in a hundred. Penny Frank of the Church Pastoral Aid Society talks about this being "the last generation for the Church." She adds that, as a result, "children in some of our estates will never cross the bridge to church attendance."[41] Ninety-six percent of children in the United Kingdom are growing up without any exposure to the church or its message. None of them will ever return to church! They might of course *come* to church for the first time, but they will not *return* to church. Attracting returnees is not a strategy for the future. The *Mission-Shaped Church* report concludes:

> The sober reality is that we do most of our evangelism, and even our church planting, among the 30 percent nearest to us—the fringe and

open[ly] de-churched. But the stark question remains: what of our mission to the remaining 60 percent of the nation? Any apostolic church that derives its nature from the apostolic (or sending) character of God has no option but to face its mission to the non-churched, even if this is at the cost of finding new ways of being and doing church to exist alongside what we do and are at present. *The task is to become church for them, among them and with them, and under the Spirit of God to lead them to become church in their own culture.*[42]

FROM ATTRACTIONAL EVENTS TO ATTRACTIONAL COMMUNITIES

In Christendom many people attended church, sometimes by legal constraint, more often by social constraint. In this context churches could legitimately speak of faithfully proclaiming the gospel, because each Sunday they had gospel-centered sermons. This is no longer the case. We cannot claim to be faithfully proclaiming the gospel to the lost through our Sunday preaching when most of the lost do not attend church. We need to do mission outside church and church events. This is something we need to *re*cover rather than *dis*cover, for the modern evangelical movement was born out of a recognition that the United Kingdom was not a Christian nation and that it needed to be evangelized outside of church buildings and services. George Whitefield and John Wesley preached the gospel in the open air because they were not welcome in church buildings and because the people they wanted to reach were not in church.

We cannot rely on business as usual. It cannot mean more of the same. It must involve a qualitative change rather than simply a quantitative change. One of the common assumptions, when people fail to turn up to church, is that we need to improve the experience of church gatherings. We need to improve the "product." We need better music, more relevant sermons, multimedia presentations, or engaging dramas. Or we need to relocate to pubs, cafes, or art centers. We need cool venues with cool people and cool music. The problem with this approach is the assumption that people will come to church if the product is better. To repeat what we said above: eighty-five million

Americans have no intention of attending a church service, and these figures are higher among young people.

It is no good blaming the lost for failing to turn up. It is no good bemoaning the drift of our nation away from Christianity. "Our persistent 'come to us' mind-set suggests that we really believe that people who refuse to come in the front door are beyond the reach of Christ."[43] A farmer cannot blame his crops if he fails to sow and reap. Sunday morning in church is the one place where evangelism cannot take place in our generation, because the lost are not there. Evangelism will not take place until we go out to connect with them where they are, where they feel comfortable, on their territory. We cannot assume people will come to us. We must go to them.

We need to do church and mission in the context of everyday life. We can no longer think of church as a meeting on a Sunday morning. We must think of church as a community of people who share life, ordinary life. And we cannot think of mission as an event that takes place in an ecclesiastical building. Of course, there will continue to be a role for special events, but the bedrock of mission will be ordinary life. Mission must be done primarily in the context of everyday life.

An everyday church with an everyday mission.

STRANGERS AND EXILES

It is still unusual to receive personal hostility because we are Christians, but we operate in a culture that is hostile to Christianity. Only last week a member of one of our gospel communities told how friends in his sports club are vitriolic about the Christian faith on their Facebook pages, apparently without sensing any incongruity with their friendship toward him. We may not often be persecuted, but we are marginalized. Faith in our culture is allowed to be privately engaging but is excluded from public life.

We need to wake up to the fact that Christians live at the margins. Our society has no time for the message of Jesus, and our allegiance to Jesus as Lord puts us on a collision course with the priorities of the culture. "Being on the margins rather than in the center will require a change of perspective, a very different mindset."[44]

STRANGERS

Peter opens his first letter by describing his readers as "God's elect, strangers in the world, scattered throughout Pontus, Galatia, Cappadocia, Asia and Bithynia." The idea that Christians are strangers in the world is a key motif in the letter. Peter calls his readers "strangers" or "foreigners" in 1:1 and 1:17 and "aliens and strangers" in 2:11.

Christians are like immigrants, foreigners, temporary residents, refugees. We do not belong. We do not have the rights of citizens. We are outsiders. We are living on the edge of the culture.

John Elliott argued that "strangers" in 1 Peter refers to the social status of Christians before their conversion. They were already outcasts who then found a home among God's people. Elliott's thesis, however, has not persuaded most commentators. "It underestimates," argues Miroslav Volf, "a new estrangement which a Christian way of life creates."[45] It also ignores the way the terms "strangers" and "aliens" were used to describe God's people in the Old Testament (Gen. 23:4; Lev. 19:34; Ps. 39:12).

In contrast to Elliott, Karen Jobes argues that "strangers" was a reference to social alienation *after* conversion.[46] She asks how Christians came to be in Asia Minor, a vast, relatively remote area for which we have no evidence of missionary activity in the first century other than the existence of churches in the locations described in 1 Peter 1:1. People have speculated that Peter himself evangelized these regions; hence the association that leads him to write this letter. But again there is no evidence for this. Jobes instead suggests that the Christians were converted elsewhere and then moved to Asia Minor where, no doubt, they continued to spread the message and gain new converts.

Jobes cites the Roman policy of colonizing conquered regions by moving people to new locations. The emperor Claudius is known to have colonized Asia Minor in this way, establishing formal Roman colonies in all the fives areas mentioned in 1 Peter 1:1. Noncitizens were sent to such regions, sometimes because they were perceived to be troublemakers in Rome. The main qualification for such deportation was that one lacked Roman citizenship, and the Latin equivalent of "foreigner" in verse 1 was a legal term referring to a free person who was not a Roman citizen. So such people were perceived as foreigners in the Roman areas from which they were sent *and* in the colonized areas to which they were sent. The most famous Roman expulsion occurred during the reign of Claudius when he expelled the Jews from Rome, including Priscilla and Aquila (Acts 18:2). Among these Jews were Christian converts, perhaps disproportionately so. Many might well have found themselves in Asia Minor where they continued to proclaim the gospel and establish churches. Moreover there is a long tradition of Peter's being based in Rome long before his later death under Nero. Peter, then, would have had personal contact with the Christians who were then deported in this way, and this would explain why he later writes to them in Asia Minor. Peter may have escaped the expulsion of Jews or, like Priscilla and Aquila (Rom. 16:3), returned after the death of Claudius. His cryptic reference to Babylon in 5:13 might be because he did not want to reveal his current location in Rome.

Jobes does not claim that this sociopolitical background negates a metaphorical understanding of the term. Rather, the two interrelate. "Peter uses the socio-historical situation of his readers to explain their socio-political situation."[47] Peter is not saying it is *as if* his readers are on the margins of society. His readers really are on the margins of society.

Whatever the merits of Jobes's historical reconstruction, the important point to highlight is that the terms "aliens" and "strangers" describe real social realities. Rather than understanding "strangers" as "describing the believer's transitory life on this earth as a journey toward their heavenly home, it should be understood primarily as defining the relationship between the Christian and unbelieving society."[48] In other words, Peter uses their experience of social marginalization to describe their experience as those in Christ. The church in Asia Minor is socially and culturally on the margins. Miroslav Volf concludes: "That the members of the Petrine community might have become Christians because many of them were socially marginalized seems an intelligent hypothesis. That they became alienated from their social environment in a new way when they became Christians is what the epistle explicitly states."[49]

Ask the government how to become a citizen, and they will tell you that you have to live in the country for a certain number of years, be of good character, and pass a citizenship test. Except, of course, that there is an easier way to become a citizen, which is to be born there. That's the way most people become citizens. It was the same in Rome. Some people could earn citizenship, but most were born as citizens.

It is the same for Christians. We are foreigners and exiles because we have been born anew into a new homeland. "Praise be to the God and Father of our Lord Jesus Christ! In his great mercy he has given us new birth into a living hope through the resurrection of Jesus Christ from the dead, and into an inheritance that can never perish, spoil or fade—kept in heaven for you" (1 Pet. 1:3–4). Peter emphasizes that we have been born *into* something: a living hope and a new inheritance. We have become citizens of a new homeland. It is not something we earned through good character or by passing a citizenship test. It happened to us by being born again.

Peter is not saying heaven is our new home. Our home is the new creation, which is "kept" in heaven for us. Our inheritance is kept for us (1 Pet. 1:4) and we are kept for our inheritance (v. 5). Many of the refugees with whom we work in Sheffield have no certainty of returning to their homeland. Indeed most of them have no reason to suppose they will ever go home and every reason to think they will not. But Christians are certain of going home to receive their inheritance. How can we be certain? Through the resurrection. Jesus has returned home ahead of us, opening up the way (v. 3). So we may be strangers now on earth, but we are not strangers in God's kingdom.

The reverse is also true: being members of another kingdom makes us outsiders here on earth. Peter says that your former friends "think it strange that you do not plunge with them into the same flood of dissipation, and they heap abuse on you" (1 Pet. 4:4). We have become strangers because we have become strange! Our values, lifestyle, and priorities are radically different from the surrounding culture. Our faith makes us strangers in our own land. We do not fit in. We are on the margins.

EXILES

In his opening description of his readers Peter not only refers to them as "strangers," but literally as "strangers of the Diaspora." "Foreigners in exile," we might say. As a noun, *Diaspora* was a technical term for Jews scattered beyond Palestine after the Babylonian exile in 587 BC. Peter's readers almost certainly include Gentile Christians, but he likens them to Jews in Babylonian exile. We are exiles.

Peter seems to be writing in the style of a Jewish Diaspora letter written from Jerusalem to Jewish exiles.[50] Indeed there are good reasons to think that his letter is modeled on a letter the prophet Jeremiah wrote back in the sixth century BC to the exiles in Babylon (Jeremiah 29). Jeremiah's letter is introduced: "This is the text of the letter that the prophet Jeremiah sent from Jerusalem to the surviving elders among the exiles and to the priests, the prophets and all the other people Nebuchadnezzar had carried into exile from Jerusalem to Babylon" (Jer. 29:1). First Peter 2:11–12 and Peter's quote from Psalm 34 in 1 Peter 3:11 seem to echo Jeremiah's call to "seek the peace and prosperity of the city to which I have carried you into exile" (Jer. 29:7). Psalm 34 is itself a psalm of exile. The Greek version of the Old Testament, which Peter uses, describes God in verse 4 as delivering David from all "his sojournings," which is related to the word "aliens" that Peter uses to describe Christians.

But here is the key thing. At the end of the letter Peter sends greetings "from Babylon" (1 Pet. 5:13)—almost certainly a cryptic reference to Rome. This is not a letter from home in Jerusalem to exiles in Babylon. This is a letter *from* exile *to* exile. Exile is not geographically defined. Christians are not strangers because they have moved from their homeland to a new country. They are exiles because their identity has so radically changed that they are no longer at home in their country of birth. The reference to Babylon reminds us of Daniel, who rose to the top of the Babylonian political system, fulfilling Jeremiah's ... to seek the prosperity of the city. We are called to get involved in the world and to bless our cities, but we cannot do so on the basis that our nation is a Christian nation. This is not our home.

HOSTILITY

Peter says his readers "may have had to suffer grief in all kinds of trials" (1 Pet. 1:6). Commentators agree that the suffering Peter's readers were undergoing was not at this point state-sponsored imprisonment or martyrdom (though that would come later). Instead it was the suspicion and censure of their neighbors. Karen Jobes says, "Because of their Christian faith, they were being marginalized by their society, alienated in their relationships, and threatened with—if not experiencing—a loss of honor and socioeconomic standing (and possibly worse)."[51] Howard Marshall says, "At this stage it seems that state action was rare . . . and that what Christians had to fear was more in the nature of social ostracism, unfriendly acts by neighbors, pressure on Christian wives from pagan husbands, masters taking it out on Christian slaves and other actions of that kind. It was sufficient, in any case, to make life uncomfortable."[52]

The hostility described throughout the letter is verbal slander and malicious accusations: "They accuse you of doing wrong" (1 Pet. 2:12); "the ignorant talk of foolish men" (v. 15); "insult" (3:9); "those who speak maliciously against your good behavior in Christ"; "slander" (3:16). "It was precisely the precarious legal status of foreigners that provided the closest analogy to the kind of treatment Christians could expect from the hostile culture in which they lived."[53] We cannot know what people said to Christians in the marketplace and street. Day to day insults are rarely written down in the historical records. But there is a famous piece of graffiti surviving from the first century that depicts a donkey on a cross with the words "Alexander worships his God." Alexander, it seems, was a Christian whose faith in a crucified Savior was being ridiculed. Christians were being slandered, excluded, and marginalized. In other words, it is much like our experience today.

AN UNSEEN LORD

Peter says of Jesus, "Though you have not seen him, you love him; and even though you do not see him now, you believe in him and are filled with an inexpressible and glorious joy" (1 Pet. 1:8). We love what we have not seen. We believe in what we cannot see.

Peter recognizes this will be received with incredulity by our unbelieving neighbors. The Roman Empire knew how to do propaganda. It knew how to project its glory and power on its subjects. Its symbols of power were everywhere: Roman standards, eagles, magnificent civic buildings. Everywhere the eye turned in the cities of Asia Minor there were signs of the triumph of Roman imperialism. The eternal city was setting itself up for an eternal reign.

It is not so very different today. We still use Romanesque architecture and symbols to express imperial power. Eagles or lions adorn our currency. Civic buildings are built with Roman columns and domes. But the power that projects itself with the greatest ubiquity is that of consumerism. Everywhere the eye turns in Western cities we see advertising, brands, logos, hoardings. It is impossible to avoid. So it is hardly surprising that its values are implanted in our lives.

All the time Christians orient their lives to a Lord they cannot see. Peter knows that is a hard thing to explain to people. We shape our lives around something we cannot see and have never seen. Peter recognizes that it makes us sound weird.

A REJECTED LORD

Peter says: "Concerning this salvation, the prophets, who spoke of the grace that was to come to you, searched intently and with the greatest care, trying to find out the time and circumstances to which the Spirit of Christ in them was pointing when he predicted the sufferings of Christ and the glories that would follow" (1 Pet. 1:10–11). The message of the Old Testament is the sufferings of Christ and the glories that would follow. Jesus sets the pattern: suffering followed by glory. We suffer hostility and marginalization just as he did. Indeed Jesus suffered the ultimate marginalization: he was pushed out of the world onto the cross. As Jesus said, "If the world hates you, keep in mind that it hated me first. . . . If they persecuted me, they will persecute you also" (John 15:18–20). Or consider the words of Hebrews:

> The high priest carries the blood of animals into the Most Holy Place as a sin offering, but the bodies are burned outside the camp. And so Jesus also suffered outside the city gate to make the people holy through his own blood. Let us, then, go to him outside the camp, bearing the disgrace he bore. For here we do not have an enduring city, but we are looking for the city that is to come. (Heb. 13:11–14)

We have become outsiders just as Jesus was an outsider. We are marginal in our culture because Jesus is marginal. The cross is the ultimate expression of marginalization and to follow him is to take up our cross daily. It is daily to experience marginalization and hostility. Being on the margins is normal Christian experience. Christendom was the aberration. Rather than assume we should have a voice in the media or on Main Street, we need to regain the sense that anything other than persecution is an unexpected bonus.

But Peter also says we "have been chosen according to the foreknowledge of God the Father" (1 Pet. 1:2). The world has "unchosen" us so that we have become the rejected and marginalized, but God has chosen us. Just as we share in Christ's suffering, so we will share in "the glories that would follow" (v. 11; 4:12–13). And God has chosen us for a purpose: "Out of all nations you will be my treasured possession," he says to his people. "Although the whole earth is mine, you will be for me a kingdom of priests and a holy nation" (Ex. 19:5–6). The doctrine of election, God's choice of us, is never intended as an indulgence. Its purpose is always mission.

We cannot only survive on the margins; we can thrive on the margins. From the margins we point to God's coming world. We offer an alternative lifestyle, values, relationships—a community that proves incredibly attractive. First Peter equips us to go back into the world—into our classrooms, boardrooms, factories, playgrounds, and changing rooms—as men and women who, like our Savior before us, are those who are marginal yet world changing.

2

EVERYDAY COMMUNITY

1 PETER 1:13-2:8

Imagine you woke up one day to discover that you had become a missionary in a foreign land. The language, the culture, the worldview, and the values are all unfamiliar. Fortunately you are part of a team. What are you going to do? Together you are going to learn the language and the culture. You are going to explore how the Bible story interacts with the outlook of the people around you. You are going to try to connect with them at a relational level.

This is the situation in which the church in the West finds itself. The culture has moved on. It is not what it was a hundred years ago when it was significantly shaped by the Bible story. We need to wake up and realize we are in a missionary situation. We cannot continue to undertake mission in a pastoral mode. We cannot assume people feel any need or obligation to attend church. We cannot even assume we understand the culture. We need to operate as missionaries in a foreign land.

WE CANNOT EXPECT THE WORLD TO BE LIKE US

A Christendom mentality expects the world to be like us and share our values. And it protests when the world is not like us. Often Christians complain about the treatment of Christianity in the wider culture. They bemoan legislation that does not reflect Christian values. They lament the representation of Christianity in the media. They decry politicians who profess themselves atheists. We do not welcome any of these things, but none of them surprise us. We cannot expect the world to be like us. Indeed we are surprised whenever we do see the culture conforming to Christian values or reacting positively to the church. The tradition of nonconformist dissent has been replaced by middle-class conformity. We need to discover or recover the sense that if this year we are not imprisoned, then it has been a good year in which by the grace of God we have gotten off lightly.

It was ever thus. In 2:4–8 Peter says believers are "like living stones" that are "being built into a spiritual house" with Jesus as the cornerstone or capstone. We are living stones like Christ the living Stone. But notice how Christ the Stone is described. He is "rejected by men but chosen by God and precious to him" (v. 4). He is "the stone the builders rejected [that] has become the capstone" (v. 7). He is "a stone that causes men to stumble" (v. 8). Peter is following Jesus himself in using Psalm 118:12 to describe his rejection by humanity (Mark 12:10). Jesus is rejected by men but chosen by God. Jesus is marginalized by the wider culture but honored by God.

The cornerstone is the stone to which all the other stones are aligned. The Stone to which we as living stones are aligned is the Stone that has been rejected by men but honored by God. So we can expect human rejection and divine honor to be our experience as well. Indeed Peter says, "Whoever believes in him will not be put to shame. So the honor is for you who believe" (1 Pet. 2:6–7 ESV).

IT IS NOT OUR CULTURE ANYMORE

In Christendom we could assume that the culture of the church was similar to the culture of the world. Or we could at least claim that it should be. Some individuals might reject the values and worldview of the church, but the culture as a whole was congruent with Christianity. To some extent this worked in both directions. The church could claim that the world should match the culture of the church. But at the same time, the church conformed to the culture of the world. This is a Christendom mentality.

We can no longer assume the wider culture matches that of the church. We can no longer assume people share a similar worldview to ours. Most people do not believe in a personal God, and most people do not believe there is only one true religion. People are biblically illiterate. We cannot talk about guilt, faith, religion, or even God and assume that people understand what we are talking about. "The gospel used to have more plausibility structures supporting it than it does today."[1] We cannot talk about Jesus and assume that people locate him in a framework of creation, fall, redemption, and future hope. Everything has to be explained.

> In a London school a teenager with no church connections hears the Christmas story for the first time. His teacher tells it well and he is fascinated by this amazing story. Risking his friends' mockery, after the lesson he thanks her for the story. One thing had disturbed him, so he asks: "Why did they give the baby a swear word for his name?"
>
> One Sunday in Oxford a man visits a church building to collect something for his partner who works during the week in a creative-arts project the church runs. He arrives as the morning congregation is leaving and recognises the minister, whom he knows. Surprised, he asks: "What are all these people doing here? I didn't know churches were open on Sundays!"[2]

These are extreme cases, but they illustrate the growing disconnection between Christianity and our culture. Many people in our Western context are a strange hybrid of secularism and pluralism. They themselves have grown up without any meaningful church contact but now live in neighborhoods with many Muslims. They believe about religions what we believe about denominations: there are real differences, but fundamentally we are the same. I have had a number of conversations in which I talk about faith in Jesus and my friends talk about "being religious." They assume we are calling them to be religious, not in the sense of law-based religious activity or morality but in a more general sense of a vague spiritual sensibility that they are free to interpret for themselves. Simply to call such people to faith in Christ as their Savior is meaningless. They do not know who Christ is, what faith is, why they need saving, or from what they need saving. They would probably interpret it as a call to neighbor love and private prayer. Tim Keller says:

> In the past, many of our neighbors could understand traditional Christian preaching even when they responded with disagreement or indifference. During the last fifteen years, however, our message is increasingly met with dumbfounded incomprehension or outrage. Until a generation ago in the US, most adults had similar moral intuitions whether they were born-again believers, church-goers, nominal Christians, or non-believers. That has changed.[3]

Claiming that the West is a mission field is now common, but there is a big gap between the rhetoric and the reality of our attitudes. One of the measures of that gap is the extent to which we are willing—or unwilling—to learn from the experience of mission and the church around the world. If we really believed we are in a mission field, then we would all be reading books written by third-world Christians and cross-cultural missionaries. We would be looking to operate as missionaries to another culture.

Let us give one example. Chronological Bible storying is an approach to pioneer evangelism and church planting that is commonly used among unreached people groups around the world.[4] Missionaries take time to understand the culture and then create a set of simplified Bible stories that cover the key turning points in the story of salvation along with Bible stories that address the barriers and bridges to belief in that culture. They then teach these stories to those who are interested. People learn the stories so they can retell them and also reflect on them together. Typically there are thirty to forty stories in a story set, and they climax with the death and resurrection of Christ. Those who are interested continue with stories in Acts to help form new believers into churches. Different story sets can also be used in discipleship and leadership training. In this way even nonliterate peoples gain a good understanding of the Bible.

This approach is widely used in many varied cultures around the world. Yet its use in the West is rare.[5] Why is this? Where it has been used, it has been successful. I once talked to a member of a church planting team who told me how valuable storying was proving with her Muslim contacts. In the same conversation she asked how she could reach the disaffected white teenagers in her church youth group. I told her how effective storying had been in engaging young people in our context. It was a eureka moment for her. She had never thought to use storying with Westerners. Among those leading the development and deployment of chronological Bible storying has been the International Missions Board of the Southern Baptist Convention. I once asked a student in a SBC Bible college whether storying was taught or used in churches in the southern States. He laughed. Our point is not to push storying (though that would be no bad thing), but to highlight the extent to which, despite our rhetoric, we do not see our context as a missionary context needing the same approaches as mission elsewhere.

Peter does not present a complex model of how we should adapt to our context. Instead he describes the new identity of his readers in a way that inevitably shapes their engagement with their neighbors in a gospel-centered way. At a number of key moments Peter says "therefore" in a way that turns identity into action, indicatives into imperatives (1 Pet. 1:13; 2:1; 4:1, 7). There are repeated references to the "walk" of Christians (1:15, 17, 18; 2:12; 3:1, 2, 16). First Peter shows how our new identity as the people of God enables us to live on the margins.

So the strangers motif is more than descriptive. It also suggests how Peter's readers are to relate to an alien culture. Think of your own encounters with another culture while on vacation or mission visits perhaps. Think how you related to the culture of the people around you. As foreigners, Christians are to treat their host culture with respect, honor those in authority, and seek its prosperity. But we will never feel at home in the culture.

Peter highlights the need for respect or honor to everyone, including those in political authority, toward wives in the home, and toward inquirers however hostile they may be in their intent (1 Pet. 2:17, 18; 3:7, 15). They are to show "fear" to masters in the workplace and husbands in the home (2:18; 3:2).

Think of a diplomat assigned to a foreign country. Her ultimate allegiance is to her homeland, but she pursues the cause of her homeland by showing meticulous respect for the culture and people of the country to which she has been assigned. Although we have been distanced from our previous culture by our new birth, we pursue the cause of our new King by showing respect to the people around us. "But in your hearts set apart Christ as Lord. Always be prepared to give an answer to everyone who asks you to give the reason for the hope that you have. But do this with gentleness and respect, keeping a clear conscience, so that those who speak maliciously against your good behavior in Christ may be ashamed of their slander" (1 Pet. 3:15–16). We set apart Christ as Lord because our homeland has changed. We proclaim the gospel to extend the rule of our Lord. But we do this with "gentleness and respect" to confound our accusers.

Citing Peter's call for gentleness (1 Pet. 3:4, 16), Croatian theologian Miroslav Volf argues for what he calls "soft difference": "Fear for oneself and one's identity creates hardness. The difference that joins itself with hardness always presents the other with a choice: either submit or be rejected." In contrast, "for people who live the soft difference, mission fundamentally takes the form of witness and invitation. They seek to win others without pressure or manipulation. . . . The soft difference is the missionary side of following in the footsteps of the crucified Messiah. It is not an optional extra, but part and parcel of Christian identity itself."[6]

REDISCOVERING THE CULTURE

Recognizing our missionary context means we can no longer assume that the church understands the culture. We need to rediscover or relearn the culture. We need to get to know our neighborhood, its people, and their stories, values, worldview, and culture. We need to ask the kind of questions that missionaries ask when they enter a new culture, questions such as:

Where?
- Where are the places and activities we can meet people (the missional spaces)?

- Where do people experience community?
- Are there existing social networks with which we can engage, or do we need to find ways of creating community within a neighborhood?
- *Where* should we be to have missional opportunities?

When?

- What are the patterns and timescales of our neighborhood (the missional rhythms)?
- When are the times we can connect with people (the missional moments)?
- How do people organize their time?
- What cultural experiences and celebrations do people value? How might these be used as bridges to the gospel?
- *When* should we be available to have missional opportunities?

What?

- What are people's fears, hopes, and hurts?
- What gospel stories are told in the neighborhood? What gives people identity (creation)? How do they account for wrong in the world (fall)? What is their solution (redemption)? What are their hopes (consummation)?
- What are the barrier beliefs or assumptions that cause people to dismiss the gospel?
- What sins will the gospel first confront and heal?
- In what ways are people self-righteous?
- What is the good news for people in this neighborhood?
- What will church look like for people in this neighborhood?

Communities are not always defined by geography. They may also be defined by ethnicity, leisure interest, time of life, and so on. In an urban context most people are part of several overlapping communities. Ask people what it's like to live in your area. If you are an insider, ask outsiders what they find weird about your community. If you are an outsider, ask insiders how they view their community.

You might ask these kinds of questions on first encountering a new community or neighborhood. But they should also be questions we ask all the time so that missional reflection is a normal part of our lives. We cannot work on our understanding of our neighborhood and then sign it off. These questions should be part of the ongoing discussions we have as gospel communities.

Hold activities such as team meetings, one-to-one mentoring, talk preparation, and reading in public spaces such as cafes, pubs, and parks. It will help you think in a missional way as you plan and prepare. If you prepare Bible teaching in a coffee shop, for example, you are more likely to find yourself developing your teaching as a dialogue with the culture. But if you simply prepare in your study surrounded by your books, then you will naturally speak into this context, addressing the concerns of professional exegetes. If you hold a leader meeting in a cafe, then you are more likely to think in missional terms as you discuss the business of the church.

In many cases you will be able to identify where community happens in your neighborhood and therefore be part of that community. The church often seems to have an obsession with doing everything itself. If you want to reach hikers, you start a church hiking group. But why not join an existing hiking group? Somebody else does all the hard work organizing the group. There may, though, be situations in which you discover there is no real community going on. Then you can become the people who bring others together.

LOVING THE CULTURE

Some of Peter's readers may have responded to hostility with passivity, keeping their heads down, keeping quiet about their Lord, and conforming to social patterns as much as possible. The equivalent today are those who hide in a ghetto or reshape Christianity into more socially acceptable forms. Others may have responded with aggression, wanting to fight back. The equivalent today are those who assert the Christian-ness of the nation and fight for Christian values to be normative within society.

Peter charts a third route: doing good in suffering, what we might call "proactive gentleness." Christians are not to become a sectarian ghetto. Instead they are repeatedly called to respond to hostility with good works (1 Pet. 2:12, 15, 20, 24; 3:1, 11, 13, 17; 4:19). It is an echo of

Jeremiah's call to the exiles in Babylon: "Seek the peace and prosperity of the city to which I have carried you into exile. Pray to the LORD for it, because if it prospers, you too will prosper" (Jer. 29:7). In Jeremiah there is even an element of self-interest. Jeremiah warns the exiles that return is not imminent, so they should seek the prosperity of the city because for the time being it is also their prosperity.

We need to love the city. Tim Keller identifies the following characteristics of a missional church:

> A "missional" small group is not necessarily one which is doing some kind of specific "evangelism" program (though that is to be recommended). Rather, (1) if its members love and talk positively about the city/neighborhood, (2) if they speak in language that is not filled with pious tribal or technical terms and phrases, nor disdainful and embattled language, (3) if in their Bible study they apply the gospel to the core concerns and stories of the people of the culture, (4) if they are obviously interested in and engaged with the literature and art and thought of the surrounding culture and can discuss it both appreciatively and yet critically, (5) if they exhibit deep concern for the poor and generosity with their money and purity and respect with regard to opposite sex, and show humility toward people of other races and cultures, (6) they do not bash other Christians and churches—*then* seekers and non-believing people from the city (A) will be invited and (B) will come and will stay as they explore spiritual issues. If these marks are not there it will only be able to include believers or traditional, "Christianized" people.[7]

It is so important to love your neighborhood and its culture. As we sense our growing marginalization with the wider culture, it is all too easy to view it as a threat. But viewing the culture around you as a threat is not a good starting point for reaching people with the gospel. Awhile back I did some research on small groups and visited a number of small-group Bible studies. In two cases, they began to speak of Muslims in their neighborhood. The language used suggested they felt they were embattled with Muslims poised to "take over." It turned out that no one had talked to the Muslim neighbors. Muslims had become a dehumanized other. This attitude rendered relationship building for the sake of the gospel all but impossible.

You might like to consider how your church community measures up against Keller's criteria. Keller says the members of a missional community "love and talk positively about the city and neighborhood." You might like to invite your missional community to identify ten things you all love about your neighborhood.

In our context we have woven a commitment to "blessing the city" into our values. We say:

> We are committed to blessing our neighbourhoods and cities—redressing injustice, pursuing reconciliation and welcoming the marginalized. We celebrate the diversity of cultures in our local contexts while recognising the need for gospel renewal. We encourage one another to glorify God and serve others through the workplace, business, community projects, government and artistic endeavour.[8]

CHOSEN TO BE DISTINCTIVE

Alongside Peter's call for positive engagement and respect is a negative counterside. Peter calls on his readers to abstain from sinful desires. "As obedient children, do not conform to the evil desires you had when you lived in ignorance" (1 Pet. 1:14). "Dear friends, I urge you, as aliens and strangers in the world, to abstain from sinful desires, which war against your soul" (2:11; see also 1:18; 4:2–3). This act of abstaining from sinful desires will bring Christians into conflict with a culture that does not restrain sinful desires (4:2–4). Our imagined diplomat's ultimate loyalty is to her homeland. So she will adapt and adopt local custom, but only insofar as they are compatible and congruent with the values of her homeland. Karen Jobes says Peter presents "the challenging principle that it is better to suffer than to sin": "First Peter challenges Christians to reexamine our acceptance of society's norms and to be willing to suffer the alienation of being a visiting foreigner in our own culture wherever its values conflict with those of Christ."[9]

Having described Christians as strangers and exiles in 1 Peter 1:1, Peter says we "have been chosen according to the foreknowledge of God the Father, through the sanctifying work of the Spirit, for obedience to Jesus Christ and sprinkling by his blood" (v. 2). Why does

Peter say these things in this order? At first sight, it seems somewhat random. It is not the list we would have put together.

It takes us back to Mount Sinai. God tells Pharaoh to free Israel, "my firstborn son" (Ex. 4:22–23). God is the Father of Israel who has chosen Israel from among all the nations to know him and worship him, and God brings them to Mount Sinai to give them the covenant with the Ten Commandments. There he calls them "a holy nation" (Ex. 19:4–6). The word *sanctified* means "made holy" or "set apart." They are called to be distinctive. They are set apart from all the nations to live under God's reign and so make God known to the nations. God sanctifies them so that there will be one place on earth where the goodness of his reign can be seen. So God's people are saved for missional obedience. The covenant is confirmed by the sprinkling of blood. "Then [Moses] took the Book of the Covenant and read it to the people. They responded, 'We will do everything the LORD has said; we will obey.' Moses then took the blood, sprinkled it on the people and said, 'This is the blood of the covenant that the LORD has made with you in accordance with all these words'" (Ex. 24:7–8).

All these elements are present in 1 Peter 1:2. We are chosen from the world by the Father, sanctified for the sake of the world by the Spirit, and called to missional obedience by the sprinkling of Christ's blood.

Peter identifies the church as the new Israel (1 Pet. 1:2, 18–19; 2:9–10). We are recapitulating the story of Israel, and Peter locates us in that story at Mount Sinai. The Israelites at Sinai were strangers going to a homeland or an inheritance they had never seen and kept en route by the pillars of cloud and fire. In the same way we are strangers going to an inheritance we have never seen and kept en route by the Holy Spirit (1:3–5). And, like Israel, we are chosen to be distinctive through obedience to God so that the world can see that God is good (1:2; 2:9–12).

Peter says, "As he who called you is holy, so be holy in all you do; for it is written: 'Be holy, because I am holy'" (1 Pet. 1:15–16). Peter is quoting from Leviticus. Leviticus can be a scary book, full of rules and regulations with which we find it hard to connect. But fundamentally the book of Leviticus is about God creating a new society through his word, which is distinctive in every way. In this way Israel will display the holiness of God in a way that attracts the nations to find blessing in God as God promised to Abraham. Leviticus is intended to create this distinctive people by shaping every aspect of life, individually and corporately. It was not just about what people did in the temple; it was about what they did in the market. This holiness knows no boundaries. It defines our friendships, marriages, work, leisure, finances, and politics. Holiness is as much about what you do on Monday morning on the factory floor as it is about what you do on a Sunday morning in a church gathering. Holiness is as much about the kind of neighbor you are as it is about the kind of church member you are. Holiness is as much about who you are when you are holding a steering wheel as it is about who you are when you are holding a Bible. Like Leviticus, Peter is going to spell out what it means for the church to be distinctive in every area of life, but the headline is: "Be holy because I am Holy." "Be distinctive because I am distinctive."

WE CANNOT EXPECT TO BE LIKE THE WORLD

The event-based approach to evangelism, which is characteristic of a Christendom mentality, is constantly trying to create experiences that match those found in the world. We want our music, our oratory, and our style to be such that people attend our meetings.

But it is a mistake to pursue relevance as an end in itself or to emphasize how we are like the world around us. For one thing, our "product" will always be inferior to that offered by Hollywood, Facebook, and Nintendo. Brits spend 20 hours a week watching television, Americans 28 hours. We are entertained by multimillion-dollar movies. We undertake sophisticated role-play and action computer games. "We are naive to think the church can compete with these stimuli through three songs and a thirty-minute sermon or drama and a worship band."[10] We cannot compete on entertainment.

At best this distracts us from the need to create distinctive communities that communicate a distinctive gospel, a gospel which more often than not grates with the wider culture. At worst the medium becomes the message, and the challenge of the gospel is lost among the entertainment or watered down to make it palatable to the audience. We have already seen that in a post-Christian context we cannot rely on church events however cool, because the majority of people will not attend church. Now we see another reason not to focus on "relevant" events. Our missional cutting edge is not events that are *like* the culture but a life and message that are *unlike* the culture.

Trying to match the world begs the question, If the church is like the world then why bother with the church? The more we become like the world, the less we have to offer. Certainly we want to avoid unnecessary offense and an off-putting experience, but what will draw people to church is always going to be what is *different* about us. "The church as an alternative community can make a powerful witness when it chooses to live differently from the dominant society at just a few key points. An important task of the church is to discern what are those key points at which to be different from the evil of the world."[11]

Difference is what we need to pursue. It is not our similarity to the world that has missionary power, but our difference. This does not mean being gratuitously different. We can certainly put people off by being culturally weird, dated, or obscure. Nevertheless, we will only attract people through gospel distinctiveness. We become relevant to our world only by being gospel centered. Os Guinness says:

> By our uncritical pursuit of relevance we have actually courted irrelevance; by our breathless chase after relevance without a matching commitment to faithfulness, we have become not only unfaithful but irrelevant; by our determined efforts to redefine ourselves in ways that are more compelling to the modern world than are faithful to Christ, we have lost not only our identity but our authority and our relevance.[12]

Even if we could produce cool church events, we would create a generation of Christian consumers who look to the church to entertain them. It would only create a consumer mentality among churchgoers. We would have a generation of Christians who move from church to church hunting experiences, looking to be entertained. Some churches would attract those who want an intellectual experience through good teaching; others would attract Christians who want an emotional experience through good corporate worship. But there would be little sense in local churches that "each member belongs to all the others" (Rom. 12:5).

People often ask us what our meetings are like in The Crowded House. We have taken to refusing to answer if we can get away with it. It misses the point of what we are trying to do. We do not propose a formula for better meetings. In fact, our meetings are very ordinary. The teaching and music are okay but nothing special. If you visited, you would probably be disappointed.

At the heart of our vision is not a new way of doing events but the creation of Word-centered gospel communities in which people are sharing life with one another and with unbelievers, seeking to bless their neighborhoods, "gospeling" one another and sharing the good news with unbelievers. The context for this gospel-centered community and mission is not events but ordinary, everyday life.

Programs are what we create when Christians are not doing what they are supposed to do in everyday life. Because we are not pastoring one another in everyday life, we create accountability groups. Because we are not sharing the gospel in everyday life, we create guest services. Because we are not joining social groups to witness to Jesus, we create our own church social groups. Please do not misunderstand. We are not against meetings or events or programs. The regular meeting of the church around God's Word is vital for the health of everything else. This is where God's people are prepared for works of service. But the works of service take place in the context of everyday life.

DIFFERENTIATED ENGAGEMENT

Richard Niebuhr famously suggested five contrasting Christian attitudes toward culture: (1) Christ against culture; (2) Christ of culture; (3) Christ above culture; (4) Christ and culture in paradox; and (5) Christ transforming culture.[13] Although a useful tool for thinking about the issues, the main problem with Niebuhr's taxonomy is that it assumes an undifferentiated definition of culture. This allows Niebuhr to accuse those within the "Christ against culture" model of being inconsistent: of rejecting civil government (Anabaptists) or fine art (fundamentalists) but adopting other cultural forms such as language, traditional learning, and agriculture. But John Howard Yoder, the leading Mennonite theologian, argues that this is precisely what Christians should be doing:

> Some elements of culture the church categorically rejects (pornography, tyranny, cultic idolatry). Other dimensions of culture it accepts within clear limits (economic production, commerce, the graphic arts, paying taxes for peacetime civil government). To still other dimensions of culture Christian faith gives a new motivation and coherence (agriculture, family life, literacy, conflict resolution, empowerment). Still others it strips of their claims to possess autonomous truth and value, and uses them as vehicles of communication (philosophy, language, Old Testament ritual, music). Still other forms of culture are created by the Christian churches (hospitals, service of the poor, generalized education).[14]

In other words, culture is not a uniform or monolithic entity. It contains within it different elements that are good and elements that are bad from a gospel perspective. Being asked to identify with one of Niebuhr's categories is a bit like being asked whether you like movies or how fast you drive your car. It depends on the movie or the road conditions, and it depends on what aspects of culture we are considering. Os Guinness and David Wells say:

> We are to live in the world in a stance of both Yes and No, affirmation and antithesis, or of being "against the world/for the world." This tension is crucial to the faithfulness of the church, and to her integrity and effectiveness in the world. . . . The Christian faith is unashamedly world-affirming, and has a peerless record in contributing to education, to philanthropy, to social reforms, to medicine, to the rise of science, to the emergence of democracy and human rights, as well as to building schools, hospitals, universities, orphanages, and other beneficial institutions. Yet at the same time, the Christian faith is also world-denying, insisting on the place of prophets as well as priests, on sacrifice as well as

fulfilment, on the importance of fasts as well as feasts, and on the place
for exposing and opposing the world when its attitudes and actions are
against the commands of God and the interests of humanity. Not sur-
prisingly, the church's constant temptation has been to relax this tension
from one side or the other.[15]

Miroslav Volf suggests that Peter's use of the alien and stranger
motif allows him to present a differentiated approach to culture. Peter
does not want Christians to define their identity simply as difference
from the culture, though he calls on them to embrace difference when
this arises. Instead he wants them to see themselves in terms of their
new identity in Christ. When Peter wants to warn Christians against
certain behaviors, "the force of the injunction is not "Do not be as
your neighbors are!" but "Do not be as you were!" Volf comments:
"When identity is forged primarily through the negative process of the
rejection of the beliefs and practices of others . . . we have to push others away from ourselves and keep them at a distance. . . . Only those
who refuse to be defined by their enemies can bless them."[16]

People often highlight the tension between Peter's calls to resist
and to submit. But Peter, argues Volf, is giving "an example of differentiated acceptance and rejection of the surrounding culture."[17] Or,
as Jobes puts it, "That is, foreigners dwell respectfully in their host
nation but participate in its culture only to the extent that its values
and customs coincide with their own that they wish to preserve. In this
way the salutation of the letter introduces a concept of differentiated
engagement with society . . . of neither full assimilation nor complete
withdrawal."[18] Tim Keller summarizes:

> Unlike models that call for a transformation of culture or that call for a
> Christendom-like alliance of church and state, Peter expects the gospel
> to always be highly offensive, never completely embraced or accepted by
> the world. This is a caution to those evangelicals and mainline Christians
> who hope to bring about an essentially Christian culture.
>
> And unlike models that call solely for evangelism and are highly
> pessimistic about influencing culture, both Peter in 1 Peter 2:12 and Jesus
> in Matthew 5:16 expect some aspects of Christian faith and practice to

be highly attractive in any pagan culture, influencing people to praise and glorify God.[19]

THE KEY DISTINCTIVE IS LOVE

Peter's call to be holy comes to a climax in 1 Peter 1:22: "Now that you have purified yourselves by obeying the truth so that you have sincere love for your brothers, love one another deeply, from the heart." We are to be distinctive, and our key distinctive is brotherly and sisterly love.

The desire to be part of the in crowd, to be accepted, is strong within us all. In part this reflects the fact that we are made in the image of the relational God. God is persons-in-community, and we are persons-in-community, so it is no surprise to find that we desire community. This is a good and godly desire.

The problem is that the desire for community with people can outgrow our desire for community with God. Being accepted by a friendship group or being respected by the culture can matter more to us than God's opinion. The Bible calls this the "fear of man" (Prov. 29:25). Our insecurities make exclusion scary. But in this age some rejection is inevitable for those who follow a crucified Lord. "May I never boast," says Paul, "except in the cross of our Lord Jesus Christ, through which the world has been crucified to me, and I to the world" (Gal. 6:14).

How, then, can we thrive on the margins? An essential part of the gospel's response is that we are not alone, not even in our marginalization. By being "in" Christ we are "in with" his people, who, though rejected by the world, are precious to God. Paradoxically, although comprised of the socially insignificant, because of who Christ is, the church is the ultimate in crowd.

It is hard for us to grasp the significance of this community identity, because we live in a radically individualistic culture. We bring this worldview with us into the church so that it shapes our understanding of the gospel. So we have a loose connection with Christians on a Sunday, but then largely we go back to living our everyday lives on our own. No wonder we struggle to thrive. Our faith is animated on Sunday mornings as we sing God's praise and hear his Word. But it limps along during the week when we live apart from the body of Christ.

We have got to allow the gospel to define our identity rather than the prevailing secular and socially fragmented story that our society tells. In Christ we have been restored to what we were originally made to be: men and women who live in community and are characterized by sincere brotherly love. This is what Peter says: "Now that you have purified yourselves by obeying the truth so that you have sincere love for your brothers, love one another deeply, from the heart" (1 Pet. 1:22).

Peter talks about our new birth into a new homeland that makes us strangers and aliens in our culture (1 Pet. 1:3). In verse 23 Peter again talks about being born anew, but this time we are reborn into *a new family*. The language of family runs through this section of the letter. We are "children" with God as our "Father" (vv. 14, 17). This comes with an obligation to display the family likeness, for we are told to be holy because God is holy (vv. 16–17). Peter goes on: "For you know that it was not with perishable things such as silver or gold that you were redeemed from the empty way of life handed down to you from your forefathers, but with the precious blood of Christ, a lamb without blemish or defect" (vv. 18–19). "Forefathers" is literally "fathers." In other words, we have been redeemed from one family tradition into another. Our family background has a big influence on our actions, but we have been set free from a destructive family background.

The two halves of 1 Peter 1:22 are not linked by "so that" (NIV), but "for" (ESV): "Having purified your souls by your obedience to the truth *for* a sincere brotherly love . . ." Brotherly love is not a by-product of purification by obedience to truth; it is its *purpose*. We have been born again *for* brotherly love. The Christian community is not a happy by-product of our salvation or a convenient help to individual Christians. We have been saved to be God's holy people, to be Christ's bride, to be a new family.

We often understand in very personal terms that Jesus died for us on the cross and celebrate this with songs littered with singular pronouns, and the gospel is certainly not less than this. The Son of God "loved me and gave himself for me," says Paul (Gal. 2:20). But the gospel is much more than this. Christ died for his people. He died so he could present his bride to himself, radiant and pure. He died so that he could be the second Adam, creating a new humanity that is righteous in him. Becoming a Christian is not simply a change of mind or lifestyle. It is about being born again into a new race.

Peter says, "Therefore, rid yourselves of all malice and all deceit, hypocrisy, envy, and slander of every kind" (1 Pet. 2:1). You cannot do these sins apart from there being other people! They are sins against others, the antithesis of love. Instead of malice we are to "love one another deeply." Instead of deceit and hypocrisy, we are to show "sincere love" (literally "unhypocritical" love). Instead of "envy" and "slander," we are to love another "from the heart" (2:1; 1:22).

The word translated "strangers" in 1 Peter 1:1, 17 and 2:11 literally means "without house" or "without home" or "without family." We are "unfamily." It is the opposite of the word that Peter uses in 2:5 to talk about "a spiritual *house*." Christians have become "without home" in the culture. Roman society was viewed as a family with Caesar as the patriarch. Their new birth meant Peter's readers had moved outside this family. They had become outsiders, homeless, unfamily. But they are being built into a spiritual home, into a new family (2:5). We are not called to live as isolated individuals alone on the margins. We are being built in a new home. We are born again into a new family.

Peter is not just talking about a Sunday morning service. He is talking about living as a community that loves one another sincerely from the heart and is deeply engaged in the lives of each one in sharing life together. He is talking about dropping in on people on the way back from work, or hanging out with people and praying after a bad day, or simply relaying a great conversation with a neighbor.

THE MISSIONAL POWER OF EVERYDAY COMMUNITY

The Christian community is not only God's survival strategy for Christians on the margins. The marginalized Christian community

EVERYDAY CHURCH

is also God's missionary strategy. We might imagine greater impact could be had from the center with the ear of the rich and famous and opportunities to exert influence upon the beautiful and powerful. But God calls us to bring him glory through an everyday community of grace (1 Pet. 2:11–12).

The Christian community demonstrates the effectiveness of the gospel. We are the living proof that the gospel is not an empty word but a powerful word that takes men and women who are lovers of self and transforms them by grace through the Spirit into people who love God and others. We are the living proof that the death of Jesus was not just a vain expression of God's love but an effective death that achieved the salvation of a people who now love one another sincerely from a pure heart.

Mission must involve not only contact between unbelievers and individual Christians but between unbelievers and the Christian community. We want to build relationships with unbelievers—not in church buildings where we feel comfortable but on their territory. We also need to introduce people to the network of relationships that make up the believing community so that they see Christian community in action. People are often attracted to the Christian community before they are attracted to the Christian message. This does not necessarily mean inviting people to Sunday services. It means introducing them to our network of relationships in the context of ordinary life: inviting both Christian and non-Christian friends around for a meal or for an evening out. So our approach to mission should involve three elements: (1) building relationships, (2) sharing the gospel message, and (3) including people in community.[20]

The church may never outperform TV shows and music videos, but there is nothing like the community life of the church. There is nowhere else where diverse people come together in the same way. There is nowhere else where broken people find a home. There is nowhere else where grace is experienced and God is present by his Spirit.

I think of my own gospel community: a dozen or so people of all ages and backgrounds, eating together on a Thursday night around the table, enjoying simple food yet relishing it as a good gift from God, celebrating together what the Spirit has been doing in our lives, praying for the needs of the world, and discussing how we can bless our neighborhood in Christ's name. There are plenty of other social groups in our neighborhood, but there is nowhere else where such a diverse people come together with a commitment to being family. It is a beautiful thing.

3

EVERYDAY PASTORAL CARE

1 PETER 1:22-2:3

"Those who dream of [an] idealized community," warns Dietrich Bonhoeffer, "demand that it be fulfilled by God, by others, and by themselves. They enter the community of Christians with their demands, set up their own law, and judge one another and even God accordingly."[1] He continues:

> [We] can never live by our own words and deeds, but only by that one Word and deed that really binds us together, the forgiveness of sins in Jesus Christ. . . . Christian community is not an ideal we have to realize, but rather a reality created by God in Christ in which we may participate. The more clearly we learn to recognize that the ground and strength and promise of all our community is in Jesus Christ alone, the more calmly we will learn to think about our community and pray and hope for it.[2]

Christians have been born again into a new inheritance that makes us strangers and aliens within the wider culture (1 Pet. 1:1–4). We are called to live on the margins. But that act of rebirth also births us into a new family (vv. 22–23), an alternative community of belonging. This new family is God's demonstration of the gospel. It is the beginning of, and pointer to, the new world that will be our inheritance.

So the gospel community matters. But this does not mean the gospel Word is less important. Quite the opposite. In 1 Peter 1:22–23, where Peter explicitly links our new birth and our new family, his emphasis is on the means by which we are born anew: *the enduring Word*: "For you have been born again, not of perishable seed, but of imperishable, through the living and enduring word of God" (v. 23). The Word gives life, and the Word continues to give life.

DO NOT TRY TO "DO" COMMUNITY

What forms and sustains Christian community is, perhaps paradoxically, not a commitment to community per se but a commitment to the gospel Word. Sometimes people place a big emphasis on the importance of community and neglect the gospel Word. Community then becomes a goal toward which we work. But Peter says human activity cannot create life that endures. An exclusive focus on community will kill community. It is only the Word of God that creates an enduring community life and love.

Peter calls on us to "love one another earnestly from a pure heart" (ESV). That is a demanding command designed to create a distinctive community, but Peter first says his readers have "purified [their] souls by [their] obedience to the truth for a sincere brotherly love" (ESV). We have been purified by the gospel for love, so love. The truth purges us of those selfish desires that conflict with love, and it is this that then enables us to love one another earnestly. Love one another deeply, says Peter, "*for* you have been born again."

This is who we are. We are members of a new family, bound together in brotherly love through the gospel of Jesus and the power of the Spirit. Once again the move is from identity to action. This command is realizable because of who we are in Christ, because of the new reality that God has produced in our lives through the gospel Word. We get rid of "all malice and all deceit, hypocrisy, envy, and slander of every kind" (1 Pet. 2:1) not through gritted teeth or extra effort. We live a life of love as we crave the spiritual milk of God's enduring Word (v. 2). We keep going back to the gospel, keep believing the gospel, keep nurturing our hearts with the gospel, and keep tasting the goodness of God in the gospel.

Notice the intensity of the language that Peter uses to describe our community life: "sincere love," "love one another deeply," "from the heart." It is often said that love is an action, not a feeling, but this is not a biblical idea. Yes, love is an action and a choice. It is also a feeling, one that is often the product of making those choices but above all a feeling that arises from our own experience of God's love to us in Christ. Dietrich Bonhoeffer notes:

> When God had mercy on us, when God revealed Jesus Christ to us as our brother, when God won our hearts by God's own love, our instruction in Christian love began at the same time. When God was merciful to us, we learned to be merciful with one another. When we received forgiveness instead of judgment, we too were made ready to forgive each other. What God did to us, we then owed to others. The more we received, the more we were able to give; and the more meagre our love for one another, the less we were living by God's mercy and love. Thus God taught us to encounter one another as God has encountered us in Christ. "Welcome one another, therefore, just as Christ has welcomed you, for the glory of God" (Rom. 15:7).[3]

AN ENDURING COMMUNITY THROUGH AN ENDURING WORD

Peter's emphasis in 1 Peter 1 is on the enduring nature of the Word of God. Human beings are born through the sperm of their father, but this perishable seed creates "a life that will quickly end" (v. 23 NLT). But Christians have been born again through the Word of their new Father, and this imperishable Word endures for eternal life: "'All men are like grass, and all their glory is like the flowers of the field; the grass withers and the flowers fall, but the word of the Lord stands forever.' And this is the word that was preached to you" (1:24–25). Human ideas, trends, fashions, and accolades are all fleeting. But the Word of the Lord stands forever, and this is the Word that was preached to us.

To grasp the point Peter is making, we need to recognize the link between verses 22 and 23 of 1 Peter. Verse 23 begins with "For." Peter intends us to draw a connection between loving one another deeply and being born through the enduring Word of God. Verses 22 and 23 are about loving one another. Verses 24 and 25 are about the enduring

Word. First Peter 2:1 is again about loving one another, and verses 2 and 3 are again about the Word. The point is this: because the Word is imperishable, the family is imperishable. We have born into this family through an imperishable Word, so it is an imperishable family. Human families perish because they break up through conflict or because they are separated through death, but our new family endures. You will always have Christians to stand by you.

This is precisely what Peter's readers need to hear, because they are now "unfamily." Earthly relationships can end in rejection. Some of Peter's readers will have been rejected by their earthly families. Many have been rejected by their former friends (1 Pet. 4:4). That is why he calls on them to love one another with a sincere and deep love. The word "deeply" (1:22) has the sense of fervent or constant. In the face of worldly rejection, we are to love one another with constancy, commitment, and loyalty.

We are to be an alternative family in which those who have become "unfamily" find a home. We are to be an alternative place of belonging for displaced exiles. The Word that gave us birth is imperishable, and so our brotherly love should be imperishable. Love these people because they will always be your people. You should not, will not, become "unfamily" from this family. The word of other people is perishable. Their loyalty is fleeting. But loyalty in the family of God is lasting because we are bound together by the imperishable Word.

What is Peter's application? It is to "love one another deeply" and to "crave pure spiritual milk" (1 Pet. 2:2) with all the desperate single-mindedness of new born babies craving their mother's milk. The Word that gave us life continues to give us life. This is the word that will sustain us. This is the word that will bind us together as we live at the margins. This is the word we should crave.

Craving the milk of God's Word is so much more than acquiring new information. Peter says we are to "crave pure spiritual milk, so that by it you may grow up in your salvation, now that you have tasted that the Lord is good" (1 Pet. 2:2–3). We are people who have acquired a taste for the goodness of God and who long to experience that taste again. In 1:23 the perishable is contrasted with the enduring Word of God. In 1:18–19 the perishable is contrasted with the precious blood of Christ. The Word of God is where we discover the precious blood of Christ, where we see the goodness of God in the cross of Jesus.

So we do not read the Bible simply to fill our minds, but to change our hearts. We do not read the Bible simply to be *in*formed, but to be *con*formed to the image of Jesus. We read the Bible to stir our affections: our fear, our hope, our love, our desire, our confidence. We read it until our heart cries out, "The Lord is good!"

Andy Mason is a church planter in a deprived neighborhood in London called World's End. He tells the local drug dealers that the Bible is a bit like the crack cocaine they sell, because, like illegal drugs, it used to be smuggled into the country. In the sixteenth century William Tyndale set about translating the Bible into English. At that time the Bible was only available in Latin, and only the clergy had access to it. Tyndale had to work abroad because of the opposition he received in England, contending with spies, assassins, and betrayal. The Bibles he printed had to be smuggled into England. Eventually Tyndale was caught, imprisoned, strangled, and burned. He gave his life so we could read the Bible in English. His translation formed much of the basis of the King James Version. I have a framed page on my wall from a 1551 edition of the Matthew-Tyndale Bible, which was the first full English Bible ever printed. It included Tyndale's translation supplemented with a translation by Miles Coverdale of those Bible books Tyndale had not yet finished.

In the eighteenth century Mary Jones saved for six years to buy a Bible. Mary was the daughter of a poor weaver in Wales. When she became a Christian at age eight, she was desperate to own her own Bible because the nearest copy was at a farmhouse two miles away. So Mary saved up for six years. Then one morning in 1800, when she was fifteen, she set out for Bala, walking 25 miles barefoot across the mountains to the home of Thomas Charles, where she could buy a Bible. Charles was so moved by her story that he established the British Society to distribute Bibles around the world. The Bible Mary

Jones walked 25 miles to get is now kept in Cambridge University Library.

William Tyndale so craved the pure spiritual milk of God's Word that he spent his life on the run before dying a martyr's death to bring that milk to the people of England.

Mary Jones so craved the pure spiritual milk of God's Word that as a child she saved up for six years and then walked 25 miles to obtain a Bible.

The sense of 1 Peter 1:13 in the original Greek is this: "Set your hope fully on the grace to be given you when Jesus Christ is revealed *by* preparing your minds for action and *by* being self-controlled." To live as God's holy children in a hostile world, we need our hope firmly set on our coming inheritance. We need an eternal perspective that looks beyond present suffering (v. 6). This requires planning. If you go mountaineering, you need to be well prepared. You cannot face the hostile environment of a remote mountain in light shoes and with inadequate supplies. And you cannot face the hostile environment of a now alien culture without preparation. We need to prepare our minds for action. We need to fill our minds with the gospel story so we have confidence in our destination. We sometimes talk of people coping with adversity through great internal reserves of strength. As Christians we need *internal reserves of hope* to live on the margins. So we need to bank deposits of hope through the Word into these internal reserves. We need to prepare our minds for action. We cannot drift into hostility. We need to be self-controlled.

Prepare your minds for action is literally "gird up the loins of your mind" (KJV). Imagine a Middle Eastern man wearing a long robe. He cannot run in a long robe because its folds will flap around his legs, so he gets ready to run by tucking his robe in around his waist. The image almost certainly recalls the night of Passover, when the people of Israel were to be ready to leave their slavery in Israel. God says: "This is how you are to eat [the Passover meal]: with your cloak tucked into your belt, your sandals on your feet and your staff in your hand. Eat it in haste; it is the LORD's Passover" (Ex. 12:11). We are like those

Israelites. We have been redeemed from an empty, enslaving way of life by the precious blood of Jesus (1 Pet. 1:18–19), and now we are heading for our inheritance (vv. 3–9). And like the Israelites we need to be ready for action.

Peter is calling us to disciplined preparation for living at the margins as we wait in hope for our new homeland. We need to fill our minds with truth and especially with the hope of the gospel. This does not happen by accident. It requires planning, forethought, and self-control.

Peter is addressing the family of God's people as a family. He is calling on them *as a family* to prepare their minds for action. Craving the Word is not primarily a solitary action to be fulfilled alone in a quiet time. This is the Word that creates and sustains family bonds. In contrast to the shifting loyalties and new hostility of former relationships, this is an enduring family created by the enduring Word. The Word created our new family, and it sustains our new family, so we are to be a Word-centered community that craves that Word.

EVERYDAY PASTORAL CARE

The remainder of this chapter explores a practical framework for creating Word-centered communities in which people speak this life-sustaining, hope-inspiring, community-building Word to one another. This framework will help equip the members of gospel communities to "speak the truth in love" to one another (Eph. 4:15).

We begin with five principles of community-based, gospel-centered, mutual pastoral care.

1) We pastor one another in everyday life.

Think about how teaching and discipleship were done in ancient Israel:

> Hear, O Israel: The LORD our God, the LORD is one. You shall love the LORD your God with all your heart and with all your soul and with all your might. And these words that I command you today shall be on your heart. You shall teach them diligently to your children, and shall talk of them when you sit in your house, and when you walk by the way, and when you lie down, and when you rise. (Deut. 6:4–7 ESV)

When they were sitting in their house, when they were walking along the road—it was done in the context of ordinary life. "When you lie down, and when you rise"—in other words, not at set times, but throughout your day as opportunities arise.

Think about how Jesus did discipleship and community: around a meal, walking along the road, reflecting on events.

Or think about Paul. In 1 Thessalonians 2:8 Paul says, "We loved you so much that we were delighted to share with you not only the gospel of God but our lives as well, because you had become so dear to us." It's about sharing the gospel of God in the context of sharing our lives.

The context for pastoral care and discipleship is everyday life. Community takes place as we do the chores, watch TV, go to work, eat meals, and so on. It is about asking others about their walk with the Lord while you do the dishes together. It is about sharing a car ride to the shops and talking about how the Spirit has spoken to you through God's Word. It is about those visiting your home and seeing how you parent your children. It is about walking the dog together and discovering a pastoral need in the course of the conversation. It is about pausing in the supermarket to pray when you learn of a need or to give thanks for answered prayer. It is about having people live with you in your home.

It does not mean anything as crass as saying, "Come over and watch us parent our children." Rather, as you share your lives with people, they will see how you live in all sorts of areas and see Christian living modeled—or see Christian grace modeled when you fail to live as you should! We have a generation of young people from dysfunctional homes who need to experience Christian families in action before they become husbands, wives, or parents.

So pastoring does not simply equal intense conversations. Our model is not the therapy session or an hour with a counselor. We are not doing a slightly different version of that. That takes pastoral care out of the ordinary and creates extraordinary interventions. Clearly, there is a place for extraordinary interventions in times of crisis, but taking pastoral care almost entirely out of the ordinary and relegating it to the extraordinary creates all sorts of problems.

Consider, for example, the need to admonish or rebuke people. Paul uses a variety of terms to describe the way we are to speak the Word into the lives of one another:

- Therefore be alert, remembering that for three years I did not cease night or day to *admonish* everyone with tears. (Acts 20:31 ESV)
- We urge you, brothers, *admonish* the idle, *encourage* the fainthearted, *help* the weak, be patient with them all. (1 Thess. 5:14 ESV)
- We proclaim him, *admonishing* and *teaching* everyone with all wisdom, so that we may present everyone perfect in Christ. (Col. 1:28)
- Let the word of Christ dwell in you richly as you *teach* and *admonish* one another with all wisdom. (Col. 3:16)
- I myself am convinced, my brothers, that you yourselves are full of goodness, complete in knowledge and competent to *instruct* [= admonish] one another. (Rom. 15:14)
- Preach the Word; be prepared in season and out of season; *correct*, *rebuke* and *encourage*—with great patience and careful instruction. (2 Tim. 4:2)
- These, then, are the things you should teach. *Encourage* and *rebuke* with all authority. Do not let anyone despise you. (Titus 2:15)

From this list we can discern three key pastoral interventions:

- We teach or instruct where people are ignorant.
- We encourage or comfort where people are fainthearted.
- We rebuke or admonish where people are wayward.

Teaching and encouraging we are comfortable with, but most of us struggle with rebuking one another.

Think about the many "one another" exhortations in the New Testament. Again and again we are told to do certain things to one another within the church: love one another, pray for one another, forgive one another, and so on. They are found across all the genres and writers of the New Testament. Together they produce the following main categories:

- Be at peace with one another, forgiving, agreeing, being humble, accepting, forbearing, living in harmony, and greeting with a kiss.
- Do not judge, lie, or grumble.

- Show hospitality to one another.
- Confess your sins to one another.
- Be kind to one another, concerned, devoted, serving, and doing good.
- Instruct and teach one another.
- Admonish, rebuke, exhort, and stir up one another.
- Comfort and encourage one another.

Which are you personally best at? And which are you worst at? What about your church community? I have done this exercise in many contexts, and universally people say that rebuking is the thing they do worst.

This is because we so often take pastoral care out of the context of everyday life and make it something exceptional and extraordinary. If you are rarely rebuked, then a rebuke is a big deal. It creates or exacerbates a sense of crisis. Rebuke becomes confrontation. That may be needed in some situations, but often it can be avoided if rebuke has become a normal part of the way we disciple one another.

Indeed everyday pastoring will often avert the need for confrontation. It offers prevention that avoids the need for cure. Hebrews 3:12–13 says, "See to it, brothers, that none of you has a sinful, unbelieving heart that turns away from the living God. But encourage one another daily, as long as it is called Today, so that none of you may be hardened by sin's deceitfulness." We are all just a few small steps away from being hardened by sin's deceitfulness. Our hearts are adept at justifying our sinful desires, so we need daily encouragement not to turn away from the living God.

Everyday pastoral care is not the same as spontaneous pastoral care. Do not idolize the spontaneous over the scheduled. People can have rather romantic notions of community as a spontaneous activity in which people hang out without much planning. Somehow community does not count in this view unless it is spontaneous. But there is nothing especially virtuous about spontaneity. When people have busy work lives, community only happens if people plan to meet together. You may have to plan to do everyday pastoral care. We all have different personalities and different life patterns. Some people may need to plan to meet with others or send a regular text or stick a reminder in their schedule. Other people will do the hanging out more. We should not value one above the other or assume our way of relating is normative. Let us celebrate the diversity within the community.

What we *do* need is gospel intentionality. Ordinary life with gospel intentionality is all well and good, but if you take out the gospel intentionality, then all you have is ordinary life—and everyone does that! We need Christian communities that saturate ordinary life with the gospel. We want "God talk" to be normal—talking about what we are reading in the Bible, praying together whenever we share needs, delighting together in the gospel, sharing our spiritual struggles—with both Christians and unbelievers.

2) *We pastor one another in community.*

The God-given context for pastoral care is the church community, not the counselor's office or the therapy session or even the minister's study. There may be a place for some of these from time to time, but the primary location for pastoral care is the Christian community. Change is a community project.

The scheduled meetings of the church and the role of a gifted pastor-teacher are clearly important. Our emphasis on ordinary life is not intended to detract from the gifts God has given to his church. It is important to note the role of more formal teaching times. Paul says, "It was [Christ] who gave some to be apostles, some to be prophets, some to be evangelists, and some to be pastors and teachers, to prepare God's people for works of service, so that the body of Christ may be built up" (Eph. 4:11–12). We meet together to be taught by gifted pastor-teachers so that we are equipped to minister to one another and together build up the body of Christ. Pastoral care is not the sole responsibility of pastors anymore than evangelism is the sole responsibility of evangelists. The role of pastor-teachers is not merely to do the pastoring but to prepare God's people for works of service. Peter calls leaders "shepherds," but he calls Jesus the "Chief Shepherd" (1 Pet. 5:2, 4). Shepherds need shepherding. They too need a community that points them to "the Shepherd and Overseer of [their] souls" (2:25).

We need to get away from the idea that a minister, in the sense of an ordained church leader, does gospel ministry in the pulpit on Sunday. In a New Testament vision of church the whole community does gospel ministry in the staff room, on the street, in the workplace, at the school gate, and in the kitchen. Here in the context of ordinary life they minister to one another and to unbelievers. The church leader is someone who is sacrificed from the front line (at least in part) to equip everyone else for the front line. The primary context of mission and community and pastoral care is everyday life.

One reason change takes place in community is that it is the only context in which pastoral care can take place on an everyday basis. All the other options offer weekly pastoral care at best. Only the shared life of the Christian community offers a context for everyday exhortation and encouragement. "Encourage one another *daily*, as long as it is called Today, so that none of you may be hardened by sin's deceitfulness" (Heb. 3:13).

3) We pastor one another over a lifetime.

We pastor one another over a lifetime. Sin runs deep in our hearts. Pastoral issues are complex. Change takes a lifetime, and so pastoral care takes a lifetime.

So we cannot expect instant change. We cannot expect to have a conversation with someone that "sorts him out." Even if you bring a measure of understanding to a situation, changing the affections of the heart and the habits of behavior will take time.

It is so important that we remember this; otherwise we will soon be frustrated. "You just need to believe the gospel" might be technically correct. But we need to recognize that the struggle to "just believe" is a lifetime struggle. "Don't be afraid; just believe," says Jesus to Jairus in Mark 5:36. But the word "just" does not mean it is easy—especially when faced with the reality of death as Jairus was!

Even when there is resolution, there will still be temptation.

Someone may rejoice in God in the face of her depression today, but tomorrow will be a new battle. Someone may come to you in tears because of something his boss said, and you may speak the gospel to his heart and his attitude may change. But next time his boss is unkind the battle will begin all over again.

It is *everyday* pastoral care that enables this *lifetime* of pastoral care. Because sin is deep-seated, we need a daily dose of truth, love, encouragement, and exhortation. Because temptation is a daily challenge, we need daily to be brought back to the beauties of the gospel.

4) We pastor one another with grace.

Here we come to the "Don't try this at home" qualification. Everyday pastoring sounds great, but please do not try it at home unless . . . In the Sermon on the Mount Jesus says:

> Do not judge, or you too will be judged. For in the same way you judge others, you will be judged, and with the measure you use, it will be measured to you. Why do you look at the speck of sawdust in your brother's eye and pay no attention to the plank in your own eye? How can you say to your brother, "Let me take the speck out of your eye," when all the time there is a plank in your own eye? You hypocrite, first take the plank out of your own eye, and then you will see clearly to remove the speck from your brother's eye. (Matt. 7:1–5)

This looks like the counter text to any notion of everyday pastoral care. Pastoral care involves some exercise of judgment or discernment, but here we are told not to judge. What about removing a speck from your brother's eye when you have a plank in your own? Does this mean we cannot do pastoral care until we have sorted out sin in our own lives? Because if it does, then we will never do it! We have just noted that change is a lifetime task.

The key is the word *hypocrite*. The person who tries to remove the speck is a hypocrite. The hypocrite in the Sermon on the Mount is a self-righteous person who does what he does to be seen by men and to establish his own righteousness (Matt. 6:2, 5, 16). Jesus will bring the sermon to a close with the challenge of two gates, two paths, and two foundations. This choice is not so much between a good life and a bad life. When you look over the sermon, the alternatives are in fact self-reliance and reliance on God, a good life lived for the wrong reasons and a good life that arises from God's grace. The sermon begins:

> Blessed are the poor in spirit, for theirs is the kingdom of heaven.
> Blessed are those who mourn, for they will be comforted.
> Blessed are the meek, for they will inherit the earth.
> Blessed are those who hunger and thirst for righteousness, for they will be filled. (Matt. 5:3–6)

Jesus goes on to say "that unless your righteousness surpasses that of the Pharisees and the teachers of the law, you will certainly not enter the kingdom of heaven" (v. 20). That greater righteousness comes from God to those who hunger for it, to those who are poor in spirit, to the broken people, to those who mourn, to those who cry to God for mercy, to those who know themselves recipients of God's grace.

So those who should not remove specks from other people's eyes are self-righteous hypocrites. If you do not pastor people out of a strong sense of God's grace—both to you and to them—then you will leave them feeling condemned, but there is no condemnation to those who are in Christ Jesus (Rom. 8:1). If you leave people feeling condemned, then something has gone horribly wrong in your pastoral care. Self-righteous people make bad pastors. At best they create legalists in their own image; at worst they leave people crushed.

This means we should allow people to respond honestly and negatively to our pastoral input. We should always speak as fellow sinners pointing to our Savior rather than to our way of life or our moral code. We should encourage 360-degree pastoring rather than top-down pastoring. We should be ready for mess and indeed welcome it.

Peter speaks of the cross as an example we should follow (1 Pet. 2:21). But there is also something unique about the cross. The heart of Peter's theology is Christ our substitute bearing our sins in our place: "He himself bore our sins in his body on the tree, so that we might die to sins and live for righteousness; by his wounds you have been healed"

(2:24; 3:18). The message of grace in the cross must be at the heart of our pastoral work.

Above all, it means our aim is not to make people moral. Our aim is for people to experience joy in Christ. Paul says, "Convinced of this, I know that I will remain, and I will continue with all of you for your progress and joy in the faith" (Phil. 1:25). The goal of Paul's ministry is joy. This is not some superficial health-and-wealth teaching. This is not about creating a comfortable, complacent life. Paul experiences joy in the midst of suffering and opposition because his delight is in Christ (Phil. 1:12–21). In Philippians 3:8 he says, "What is more, I consider everything a loss compared to the surpassing greatness of knowing Christ Jesus my Lord, for whose sake I have lost all things. I consider them rubbish, that I may gain Christ." Paul's radical commitment to Christ arises from his delight in Christ, and that is the pattern for our pastoral care. We are not in the business of cajoling people into commitment. Our job is to give people such joy in Christ that the treasures and temptations of this earth look like pathetic alternatives. This leads to our fifth principle.

5) *We pastor one another with the good news.*

By *good news* we mean the gospel—the message of the lordship of Jesus, his saving death on our behalf, eternal life through his resurrection, the welcoming grace of God, the transforming power of the Holy Spirit, the care of the heavenly Father, and so on. Stick with the term *good news* for a moment. Our pastoral inventions must all offer good news. When we talk with people, they need to leave thinking, *That is such good news. I'm so relieved.* Of course in reality pastoral care is never quite that straightforward, but our goal is to offer good news that brings joy. That is the test of gospel pastoring. Is it good news? Is it gospel good news?

What else might it be?

First, it might be positive thinking but not good news. That is the sum of a lot of modern secular counseling. "You deserve it." "You can do it." "Life is not against you." It is a call to break out of negative thinking. There is something in this approach. In many ways it is the best the secular world has to offer, and often it is effective. The problem is that sometimes negative thinking is right!

I am pastoring someone at the moment who is being told by her counselor that she deserves to get better. Now, I sympathize with her because she suffers from a condition in which people punish themselves. But does she deserve to get better? She does not think so; she knows she deserves God's judgment. But I can speak real good news to her: she deserves judgment, but Jesus has taken the judgment she deserves, paid it in full, and given her the reward that he deserves so that now she is a child of God. She does not need to punish herself, because the punishment was paid in full at the cross. That is good news without any pretending. So we need to be careful not to offer positive thinking in place of the real good news.

Second, such counsel might be good advice, but it is not good news. It is all too easy, especially with broken people, to give a stream of advice. "Maybe you should buy cheaper, nonbranded products." "Maybe you should spend less time with that person." "Maybe you should feed your kids food with less additives."

The problem with such advice is twofold. First, it distorts your relationship with those to whom you offer it. If you are not careful, it puts you into the role of a parent. Or it portrays you as a together person so that others need to become like you. Second, it is not gospel. At best it might lead to reform, but it will not reconcile anyone to God or change hearts.

There is a place for advice; it can be an act of love. But we need to spell out for people the nature of what we are saying, especially if we are in a position of authority within the church. We need to distinguish between advice and gospel because they carry very different levels of authority. Advice comes with the authority of my accumulated wisdom such as it is. The gospel comes with the authority of God, and that is a very different proposition. So we need to be careful not to offer good advice in place of proclaiming the good news.

Third, we can proclaim law instead of good news. You would

think good evangelical, justification-by-faith people would not do this, but we do! Law says, "You should . . ."—You should not sleep with your boyfriend; You should read your Bible every day; You should not get drunk; You should witness to your friends; You should not lose your temper. Does any of that sound familiar? That is not good news, not to someone struggling with those issues. It is condemnation.

What the gospel says is this: "You need not . . ."—You need not get drunk, because Jesus offers a better refuge; You need not lose your temper, because God is in control of the situation. That is good news! Sin makes promises. The gospel exposes those promises as false promises and points to a God who is bigger and better than anything sin offers. That is good news.

FOUR LIBERATING TRUTHS FOR THOSE WE PASTOR

To help pastor our own hearts and to pastor one another, we want to highlight four liberating truths about God. Most of our sinful behavior and negative emotions arise because we are not believing one of these four truths as we should. Behind every sin is a lie about God. In Romans 1:24–25 Paul says:

> Therefore God gave them over in the sinful desires of their hearts to sexual impurity for the degrading of their bodies with one another. They exchanged the truth of God for a lie, and worshiped and served created things rather than the Creator—who is forever praised. Amen.

We exchange the truth about God for a lie. And because we do not believe in God as we should, something else comes to matter more to us than God. Sin is always the result of misplaced affections. Sin makes promises. When we believe those promises, we think sin offers more than God. This lie warps our affections. Our love, our delight, our fear, and our hope become misplaced.

This does not necessarily mean that we are heretics or untaught. We are not talking about confessional belief, but functional belief. Most of our problems arise not because we need new truth that we do not yet have (though sometimes this is the case), but because we need truths we already know pushed down into the everyday realities of our lives. We need to feel in our hearts the truth we already know in our heads.

So our role as those committed to pastoring one another is to speak the truth to one another in the everyday realities of our lives. If we can identify the lie behind the sin, then we can speak the truth more effectively into others' lives. This is the truth that will, as Jesus promised, set them free. We need to ask ourselves: What is the lie and what is the corresponding gospel promise? What is substituting for Jesus and what is the corresponding truth about Jesus that offers hope? The following four liberating truths about God ("four Gs") target nearly all our sinful behavior and negative emotions.[4]

1) God is great, so we do not have to be in control. We often want to be in control, so we dominate, manipulate, or overwork people. Or we fear things being out of control, so we worry. But God is sovereign. He is in control. Things may not always go the way we want, but God is in control, and he uses everything that happens to us for our good.

2) God is glorious, so we do not have to fear others. We often sin because we crave the approval of other people or fear their rejection. The Bible calls this the "fear of man" (Prov. 29:25). We live to please other people, or we are controlled by peer pressure. The Bible's answer is the fear of God. God is the glorious one whom we should fear. He is the one whose approval matters most, and he is the one whose approval we have in Jesus Christ.

3) God is good, so we do not have to look elsewhere. Sin often leads to pleasure, but its pleasures are empty and temporary. Only God brings true and lasting joy. The pleasures of sin are quick and immediate. So we need faith to turn to God for lasting joy.

4) God is gracious, so we do not have to prove ourselves. Many people act out of a desire to prove themselves. On the surface they may look impressive because they achieve many things or live good lives, but when things go well they are proud, and when things go badly they are crushed. They may look down on others because this makes them feel better about themselves or become bitter when their hard work is not rewarded in the way they want. It is also this desire that makes us determined to win an argument. The good news is that, while we can never justify ourselves before God, God has justified us through Jesus Christ. Jesus has done it all, so we have nothing left to prove.

People might get angry because they do not believe that *God is great*, that he is in control. They may believe in the providence of God in theory, but in practice they are not trusting God to provide for their needs. So when things go wrong they get angry. They feel the need to be in control, and when life is not under their control (as will be the case sooner or later), they get angry.

Or they may be angry because they do not believe that *God is glorious*. Of course, on Sunday they sing that he is robed in majesty, but on Monday morning their boss is the one they fear. Their boss looms large in their mind, eclipsing God. They are desperate for the approval of their boss, so when they have a bad day or a colleague lets them down, they become angry. The anger is an expression of their fear. The biblical answer is not to try to fear their boss less but to fear God more—to see God in his glory, majesty, holiness, love, and beauty so that God eclipses their boss. That is the word we need to speak to them.

Or they may be angry because they do not believe *God is good*. They are not looking to God for satisfaction, so they look elsewhere— to their work, their leisure, their family, their possessions, their girl- friend, or the girlfriend they wish they had. And if any of those things are threatened, they become angry.

Or they may be angry because they do not believe *God is gracious*. Maybe they have a contractual view of their relationship with God. They think that if they live an obedient life then God will bless them. They give up things for God and think God owes them in return. They may have a particular blessing in mind. They may long for a husband and think God will provide one if they live a good life. When God does not provide the blessings they want, they become embittered. They may not articulate that as anger against God; it may be an ill-defined resentment, or they may lash out randomly at people. But underneath it all is an anger against God. They need to rediscover the grace of God. God does not treat us on a contractual basis. Or, rather, he does, but that contract is the new covenant under which he forgives our sins on the basis of the blood of his Son. We do not get what we deserve, because what we deserve is hell. What we get instead is God himself.

Speaking these truths does not mean simply saying, "You just need to fear God more." These truths are not to be wielded like accusations along the lines of "Your problem is you don't believe God is great." That is not good news. Instead we are called to portray God to one another in all his glory and beauty and majesty. It means singing songs and telling stories that speak of his glory and then making the connections to everyday life. It means presenting the truth in a way that captures the imagination. The framework of these four liberating truths is just a diagnostic tool kit. Do not be satisfied with repeating the bald statements that God is great, glorious, good, and gracious. Draw upon all your knowledge of the Bible story, all the texts you have memorized, and all the hymns and songs you know to express these truths with color and texture.

Notice, too, how a symptom (in this case anger) does not automatically equate to one specific truth. People are complicated. What is more, they have all sorts of issues going on in their hearts at the same time. The heart is deceitful above all things. We will need to explore presenting issues with people to discern their underlying issues. Misplaced affections are rarely revealed on Sunday mornings when people are on their best behavior. That is why sharing life in the context of everyday life is so vital. This is when our hearts are revealed: when we face the pressures of life or in our interaction with other people in the Christian community with whom we find it hard to live.

But here is comforting news. Speaking the truth about God will do no harm. You may not precisely identify what is going on in others' hearts. If they need to hear that God is gracious, and you remind them that God is great, then you may not get it right, but you will not get it wrong! No one will be damaged by being reminded that God is their heavenly Father or that he is gracious.

What is more, while we may not be able to discern the inner workings of a person's heart, God's Word does its own analysis:

> The word of God is living and active. Sharper than any double-edged sword, it penetrates even to dividing soul and spirit, joints and marrow; it judges the thoughts and attitudes of the heart. Nothing in all creation is hidden from God's sight. Everything is uncovered and laid bare before the eyes of him to whom we must give account." (Heb. 4:12–13)

The Spirit of God is the counselor. When we speak the Spirit-inspired Word of God, the Spirit uses that Word to search the heart and counsel the heart. "The law of the LORD is perfect, reviving the soul. The statutes of the LORD are trustworthy, making wise the simple" (Ps. 19:7).

FOUR LIBERATING TRUTHS FOR THOSE WHO PASTOR

These four liberating truths are great to apply to those we pastor, but it is important also to apply them to ourselves *as pastors*. For the most part, our pastoral interventions go wrong not because we lack technique or knowledge or experience. The main reason our pastoral interventions go wrong is that *we as pastors* have failed truly to believe one of these four truths about God. To state the obvious, there are two sinners involved in any pastoral relationship; the person with the presenting issue is not the only one in the relationship with issues!

So consider the implications of our not believing these four truths as we pastor others.

1) God is great, so we do not have to be in control.

Effects of a faithless response. We will be over-controlling, the arbiter of truth. We will want immediately to correct every error for fear people might go astray or that we might lose control, so we do not give people time to grow. When we speak truth to people's lives, we will be intense and overbearing because we want to solve the problem. We fear what might happen to others, so we talk at them. We do not give them space to change or to disagree.

Also, we might become risk averse. We will not take risks with people or situations because we fear things will go wrong. We might be indecisive, because we fear making the wrong choice. We might slip into a form of clericalism in which we will not trust others to do God's work because we fear they might do it wrong, or we may micromanage.

Effects of faithful response. Our pastoral care will be relaxed and patient. We will give people space to change and time to grow. When we talk with people, we will not feel the need to sort everything out in one go. We will give them a chance to talk and space to disagree. At the same time, we will be able to take risks because we trust the outcomes to God's sovereign care. We will give away power and responsibility because we do not think everything depends on us.

2) God is glorious, so we do not have to fear others.

Effects of a faithless response. If not trusting the greatness of God leads to over-pastoring, then not fearing our glorious God will lead to under-pastoring. If we fear people more than we fear God, then we might be reluctant to speak the truth. We will not confront people because we are worried they might dislike us or reject us. We might avoid difficult decisions to prevent upsetting people. Or we might second guess what people are thinking, because we are trying to anticipate what will please them. In discussions a fearful person will often glance at others to gauge their reaction.

Or we might treat sin not in relation to a holy God but in terms of what others think of it. In other words, respectability will matter more than holiness. We will treat public sins more seriously than other sins because we are driven by people's opinions.

Another potential symptom is that we gravitate toward activities that are up front. If our goal in ministry is to be admired, people's opinions will matter more than God's opinion. We become a slave to praise. Or there is a gap between our public and private persona. The holiness that matters to us is public holiness.

Effects of faithful response. If we believe God is glorious and that he is to be feared, then we will not be controlled by other people. Only then, in fact, are we truly free to serve them in love. When we are controlled by the opinions of others, we do for them so we can win their good opinion. Our actions are self-serving. Our aim is a good reputation. Only when the glory of God sets us free from the fear of man can we serve others in love. Then we are free to speak the truth people need to hear, not what they want to hear, and we ourselves can be vulnerable before others, rejoicing in God's vindication or justification.

3) God is good, so we do not have to look elsewhere.

Effect of a faithless response. If we do not believe that God is good and the one who truly satisfies, then we might be reluctant to serve, do the minimum, or serve begrudgingly or with a sense of compulsion. We may view ministry as a burden. People might find us unapproachable because they pick up signals that we do not want to be bothered. We may look for satisfaction in other things or not stick to tasks we dislike or always move on to a new thing. We will not do the hard work of pastoral care; we will not do the hard work of hanging out with people we are not naturally attracted to or challenging people's behavior. We will avoid difficult conversations and messy people. Instead we will be interested in doing only what is fun.

Effects of faithful response. If, however, we find joy in God, then we will serve with passion and enthusiasm. We will be characterized by generosity, simplicity, and energy. Our lives will be winsome and welcoming.

4) God is gracious, so we do not have to prove ourselves.

Effects of a faithless response. We might find our identity in ministry rather than in Christ and so overwork or make others guilty through our high expectations. Or we might envy others whose ministry is more successful or take pride in our success. We ourselves will take criticism badly, being defensive or defeated, because our identity is tied up in our achievements and not in Christ's achievements on our behalf. There is a danger that our lives can become so busy and stressed because we are trying to prove ourselves that we do not model good news to people.

We will be functional legalists who think behavior matters more than motives, who want to avoid mess in favor of respectability, or who condemn those who do not measure up. We will impose a set of expectations on other people that wear them down under the weight of joyless duty. If we do not believe God is gracious, then we will not want our sins to be exposed, so we may not ask people hard questions about their spiritual life for fear of being asked in return.

Effects of a faithful response. If we rest on the grace of God and find our identity in Christ, then our lives and ministry will be characterized by peace and rest, joy and freedom, confidence and humility, compassion and kindness. We will not rejoice when others fail. Our concern will be to bless rather than to impress. We will not need the affirmation of other people, and we will be free from the need to defend ourselves. There will be a transparency and vulnerability about our lives because we do not feel the need to hide our sin. We will create a context in which other people feel able to share their struggles. Use Table 3.1 to examine your pastoral care.

Table 3.1

Is your pastoral care shaped by confidence in the four Gs?	Contrary Indicators
God is great, so we do not have to be in control	You are overbearing You are inflexible or risk averse You are impatient with people You avoid responsibility
God is glorious, so we do not have to fear others	You avoid confrontation You crave approval You behave differently around certain people You pretend or hide your true self
God is good, so we do not have to look elsewhere	You feel ministry is a burden You often complain You make people feel a burden of duty You don't stick at things
God is gracious, so we do not have to prove ourselves	You take criticism and failure badly You find it hard to relax You are proud or envy the success of others You make people feel guilty

Most poor pastoral care comes down to either over-pastoring or under-pastoring. *Over-pastoring* is a tendency to dominate or manipulate or to be overbearing and too intense when we speak. *Under-*

pastoring is a failure to challenge when we should or an avoidance of difficult people and conversations. A failure to believe that:

- God is great leads to over-pastoring (we think people need us to save them);
- God is glorious leads to under-pastoring (we fear how people will respond to us);
- God is good leads to under-pastoring (we avoid difficult situations);
- God is gracious leads to over-pastoring (we try to prove ourselves by rescuing people).

Do you see yourself in any of the descriptions of pastors whose pastoring goes awry because they do not trust God's greatness, glory, goodness, or grace? Do you have a tendency to over-pastor or under-pastor? The point is not merely to correct our behavior ("I tend to over-pastor so I need to restrain myself more"). No, the point is to see, believe, embrace, and delight in the truth about God. If you over-pastor because you do not trust God's sovereign care, then focus on God's sovereign care. Meditate on your heavenly Father; meditate on his care of creation; meditate on the gift of his Son; meditate on the mysterious sovereignty of the cross. Invite others to challenge you to trust his sovereignty and speak to you often of his greatness. Then the truth will set you free to be a good pastor.

4

EVERYDAY MISSION

1 PETER 2:9–3:16

The church is the people of God called to display the goodness of his reign to the world. It is the bride of Christ formed through his reconciling death. It is the community of grace united by the empowering presence of the Holy Spirit. Church is not so much about how we structure ourselves, where we meet, how often we meet, or even what we do when we meet. Church is about who we are as the people of God, living distinctively by grace through the Spirit under the reign of King Jesus to the glory of our heavenly Father. These are the elements that should preoccupy us. Everything else then becomes a way of presenting, harnessing, and protecting this.

Understood in this way, it is easy to see why church planting is so important. The church is God's primary mission strategy in the world. Our strategy must be to litter the world with communities of light. This encapsulates God's eternal purpose, at the heart of which are Christ and his people.

EVERYDAY MISSION

One of the central contentions of this book is that our marginal status as Christians in the West requires us to think differently about mission. One way is by dropping our preoccupation with church.

If words are defined by usage rather than etymology, the contemporary usage of *church* means we are almost certainly miscommunicating when we use it. In our culture we learn from an early age that *church* is a building. Or we see it as an institution, a relic of a bygone age, an organization in terminal decline. Nick Spencer and Graham Tomlin claim, "The most important social fact about the church is that it is an institution, and institutions are deeply unpopular in modern Britain."[1] It does not help that many Christians function as if *church* is a meeting, an event that we attend and to which we invite people. Or we think of it as an entity with structures such as constitutions, ministers, elders, committees, and so on. If we fail to understand what it means to be *church*, then we will struggle to understand what it means to follow Jesus.

This matters. If anything is a hindrance to people being introduced to Jesus, then it must be disposed of. Yes, the cross offends; Christ crucified will always be a stumbling block. But we must remove every other offense. We must do all we can to live in a way that exposes and manifests the true nature of the cross.

So this is a plea, not necessarily to ditch the word *church* (though William Tyndale replaced it with *congregation* in his translation of the Bible into English) but to be preoccupied with being that which the term truly designates. This is not some misguided interest in rediscovering the purity of a New Testament model, as if the New Testament presents one, definitive blueprint. Instead, it comes out of a passion for others to discover the grace that comes to us in Christ.

Peter says, "You are a chosen people, a royal priesthood, a holy nation, a people belonging to God, that you may declare the praises of him who called you out of darkness into his wonderful light. Once you were not a people, but now you are the people of God; once you had not received mercy, but now you have received mercy" (1 Pet. 2:9–10). He describes the church using a litany of Old Testament allusions, particularly to Exodus 19:4–6; Isaiah 43:20–21; and Hosea 2:23 (see Table 4.1). Old Testament citations in the New Testament are like hypertext links. You click on them to discover more than first meets the eye. They are not random similarities but usually indicate substantive theological background material. Verses 9 and 10 are no exception.

Table 4.1

1 Peter 2:9–10	Main Old Testament Allusions
You are a chosen people,	my chosen people (Isa. 43:20 ESV)
a royal priesthood,	a kingdom of priests (Ex. 19:6)
a holy nation,	a holy nation (Ex. 19:6)
a people belonging to God,	my treasured possession (Ex. 19:5); my people (Isa. 43:20)
that you may declare the praises of him who called you . . .	that they might declare my praise (Isa. 43:21 ESV)
Once you were not a people, but now you are the people of God;	I will say to Not My People, "You are my people" (Hos. 2:23 ESV)
once you had not received mercy, but now you have received mercy.	I will have mercy on No Mercy (Hos. 2:23 ESV)

Exodus 19:4–6 contains the words God spoke to Israel at Sinai to introduce the Mosaic covenant. As he is about to give his people the Ten Commandments, he tells them how they should see themselves and outlines the purpose of the covenant. Israel is called to be a priestly kingdom. Ordinarily priests made God known to the people and offered sacrifices. Now the whole of Israel as a community is to be priestly: making God known to the nations and calling the nations to find atonement through sacrifice. Peter's reference to a royal priesthood is more than an affirmation of the Reformation doctrine of the priesthood of believers (though in the light of 1 Peter 2:5 it is certainly not less than this). Peter is talking about our corporate identity as God's priestly people whose life together commends the goodness of his kingdom. Similarly, God's people are to be a holy or distinct nation just as God himself is holy. God is carving out one place on earth where the goodness and freedom of his kingdom can be seen. In other words, the community of God's people is to be a missional community. The law is missional in intent, defining the distinctive community life that will draw the nations to God.

The same missional ideas are present in Isaiah 43. Isaiah is looking ahead to the exile of God's people in Babylon, an exile in which Peter sees his readers (1 Pet. 1:1; 5:13). Exile was the curse that Moses warned would fall if Israel failed to be a light to the nations through faithfulness to the covenant (Deut. 28:49–68), but Isaiah says God is going to lead them home through a new exodus. The One who brought his people through the Red Sea, led them through the desert, and gave them water to drink is "doing a new thing" (Isa. 43:16–20). Peter has already described the death of Jesus as a new Passover (1 Pet. 1:18–19). Now God's redeemed people are again to declare his praises.

This calling on God's people to attract the world to God through the quality of their life is precisely how Peter goes on to apply his allusions to the Old Testament: "Dear friends, I urge you, as aliens and strangers in the world, to abstain from sinful desires, which war against your soul. Live such good lives among the pagans that, though they accuse you of doing wrong, they may see your good deeds and glorify God on the day he visits us" (1 Pet. 2:11–12).

The word *church* is first used of God's people when they are gathered at Mount Sinai. The Greek version of the Old Testament uses the word *ecclesia* in Deuteronomy 9:10; 10:4, and Stephen uses *ecclesia* to describe Israel at Sinai in Acts 7:38. Gathered around Mount Sinai the church is told to live in such a way that it will commend God to the nations. In 1 Peter 2:9–12 Peter again brings us to Mount Sinai, and again we are called to commend God to the nations through our lives.

Peter also seems to have in mind the words of Jesus when he was talking to his newly formed messianic community (Matt. 5:14–16). Our community life gives both substance and credence to our words. It is the means by which our commendation of God's glory and grace are vindicated. We are to live in the midst of an antagonistic world so that others will ask the reason for our hope (1 Pet. 3:15).

This is the mission strategy Peter gives to marginalized congregations living in a hostile context. Respond to hostility with good deeds. Live such good lives that people glorify God. At the heart of this mission strategy are not services, courses, programs, and activities but ordinary lives lived for God's glory. Mission takes places not through attractional events, but through attractional communities.

This does not mean that good works on their own are sufficient. Proclamation matters. We are called to "declare" God's praises (1 Pet. 2:9). We are to be ready to give "an answer to everyone who asks you to give the reason for the hope that [we] have" (1 Pet. 3:15). The gospel is a word, but the primary context in which that word is proclaimed is everyday life.

First Peter 2:11–12 is just the headline. Peter then goes on to apply this mission strategy to our life in society (vv. 13–17), in the workplace (vv. 18–25), and in the home (3:1–7). In each case Peter addresses those who face hostility because they follow Christ. The person who receives "unjust suffering because he is conscious of God" is a reference to someone suffering as a Christian" (2:19).[2] While Peter's words apply to the witness of all wives, his focus is on those whose husbands "do not believe the word" (3:1). In each case we are called to good works (2:15, 20; 3:1–2) and to show submission and have respect for others (2:13, 17, 18; 3:1–2). Peter also repeats his reminder that our fear of God liberates us to serve others in the face of hostility (2:17; 3:6). Centrally, there is a repeated expectation that, echoing 2:12, our good works will have a missional impact: "For it is God's will that by doing good you should silence the ignorant talk of foolish men" (2:15); "They may be won over without words by the behavior of their wives" (3:1). Interestingly, although we may think the husband's traditionally more dominant role might mean unbelieving wives are more likely to be converted through their believing husbands, research by John Finney found that unbelieving husbands are more likely to be converted by believing wives, which would appear to bear out the hope of 1 Peter 3:1–2.[3]

Notice where mission takes place: in the neighborhood, in the workplace, in the home—not in the meetings of the church. We reach a hostile world by living good lives in the context of ordinary life. Everyday mission.

It is not simply that ordinary Christians live good lives that enable them to invite friends to evangelistic events. Our lives *are* the evangelistic events. Our life together is the apologetic. There is a place for meetings at which the gospel is clearly proclaimed, but let us affirm and celebrate ordinary Christians living ordinary life in Christ's name. This is the front line of mission. Mark Greene says:

The vast majority of Christians feel that they do not get any significant support for their daily work from the teaching, preaching, prayer, worship, pastoral, group aspect of local church life. No support for how they spend 50 percent of their waking lives. As one teacher put it: "I spend an hour a week teaching Sunday school and they haul me up to the front of the church to pray for me. The rest of the week I'm a full-time teacher and the church has never prayed for me. That says it all."[4]

When we think of evangelism, we should not first think of guest services, evangelistic courses, street preaching, or door knocking. We should think of Gary at a meeting of the residents' association. We should think of Hannah in her office. We should think of Sharon serving a meal to her husband.

Here is an exercise to help identify opportunities for everyday mission.[5] Think of all the activities, however mundane, that make up your life: (1) *daily routine* (traveling to work, eating meals, doing chores, walking the dog, playing with the children); (2) *weekly routine* (grocery shopping, watching favorite television programs, exercising); and (3) *monthly routine* (gardening, getting a haircut, going to the movies). You should have a long list of activities. For each one, ask whether you could add: (1) *a community component* by involving another member of your Christian community; (2) *a missional component* by involving an unbeliever; and (3) *a gospel component* by identifying opportunities to talk about Jesus.

Clearly not everything you do can be done with someone else, but this exercise reveals just how many opportunities we do have in everyday life. You might knock on a friend's door as you walk the dog to see if he wants to walk with you. You might offer an elderly neighbor a car ride when you drive to the supermarket. You might meet a member of the Christian community for breakfast one morning each week or agree to ride the same bus. Instead of reading your Christian book in the lunchroom, you might take the opportunity to get to know your colleagues. None of this is adding anything to your schedule, for these are all activities in which you are already engaged. One of the things people in my gospel community do, for example, is watch certain television programs together, such as *The Apprentice* or *Britain's*

Got Talent, that are, in any case, best watched with a group. Invite Christians and non-Christians to watch them with you. You are going to be watching the program anyway, so why not watch it with other people, share the experience, and see what opportunities this presents?

Leave the house in the evenings. Sounds simple? Yet you know how it is, especially in the winter. It has been a tiring day at work, and it is a dark, cold evening. The easiest thing is to slump in front of the television or surf the Internet or play on the Xbox. Get out. It does not matter where you go as long as you go with gospel intentionality. Walk out the door and then decide what to do! Drop by the home of another member of your missional community. Pop around to visit a friend. Take a cake to a neighbor. Attend a local community group. Go to the theater. Hang out in a cafe. Go for a walk with a friend.

Jonathan Dodson from Austen City Life in Texas suggests eight easy ways to be missional.[6] "Missional," he comments, "is not an event we tack onto our already busy lives. It is our life. Mission should be the way we live, not something we add onto life. . . . We can be missional in everyday ways without even overloading our schedules." Here are his eight suggestions:

1) *Eat with non-Christians.* We all eat three meals a day. Why not make a habit of sharing one of those meals with a non-Christian or with a family of non-Christians? Go to lunch with a co-worker, not by yourself. Invite the neighbors over for family dinner. If it's too much work to cook a big dinner, just order pizza and put the focus on conversation. When you go out for a meal, invite others. Or take your family to family-style restaurants where you can sit at a table with strangers and strike up conversations. . . . Have cookouts and invite Christians and non-Christians. *Flee the Christian subculture.*

2) *Walk, don't drive.* If you live in a walkable area, make a practice of getting out and walking around your neighborhood, apartment complex, or campus. Instead of driving to the mailbox, convenience store, or apartment office, walk to get mail, groceries, and stuff. Be deliberate in your walk. Say hello to people you don't know. Strike up conversations. Attract attention by walking the dog . . . [or] bringing the kids. Make friends. Get out of your house! . . . Take interest in your neighbors. Ask questions. . . . Pray as you go. *Save some gas [and] the planet.*

3) *Be a regular.* Instead of hopping all over the city for gas, groceries, haircuts, [meals], and coffee, go to the same places. Get to know the staff. . . . Go at the same times. Smile. Ask questions. Be a regular. I have friends at coffee shops all over the city. My friends at Starbucks donate a ton of leftover pastries to our church [two or three] times a week. We use [them] for church gatherings and occasionally [to] give to the homeless. Build relationships. *Be a regular.*

4) *Hobby with non-Christians.* Pick a hobby that you can share. Get out and do something you enjoy with others. Try . . . local rowing and cycling teams. Share your hobby by teaching lessons. Teach sewing . . . , piano . . . , violin, guitar, knitting, [or] tennis. Be prayerful. Be intentional. Be winsome. Have fun. *Be yourself.*

5) *Talk to your co-workers.* How hard is that? Take your breaks with intentionality. Go out with your team or taskforce after work. Show interest in your co-workers. Pick four and pray for them. Form moms' groups in your neighborhood and don't make them exclusively non-Christian. Schedule play dates [for your kids] with the neighbors' kids. *Work on mission.*

6) *Volunteer with nonprofits.* Find a nonprofit [organization] in your part of the city and take [one] Saturday a month to serve [there]. Bring your neighbors, your friends, or your small group. Spend time with your church serving your city. Once a month. *You can do it!*

7) *Participate in city events.* Instead of playing Xbox, watching TV, or surfing the net, participate in city events. Go to fundraisers, festivals, clean-ups, summer shows, and concerts. Participate missionally. Strike up conversation. Study the culture. Reflect on what you see and hear. Pray for the city. Love the city. *Participate with the city.*

8) *Serve your neighbors.* Help a neighbor by weeding, mowing, building a cabinet, [or] fixing a car. Stop by the neighborhood association or apartment office and ask if there is anything you can do to help improve things. Ask your local police and fire stations if there is anything you can do to help them. Get creative. *Just serve!* [7]

LOVE JESUS, LOVE PEOPLE, LOVE LIFE

Everyday mission is not a technique or program. You cannot program unprogrammed church! We cannot offer you five steps to get your church doing everyday mission. The core elements are loving Jesus, loving people, and loving life.

Love Jesus. Enthusiasm for evangelism does not begin with evangelism at all. Exhortations to evangelize just leave us feeling useless. Driven by guilt we try turning the conversation at work around to spiritual things with horrible, crunching gear changes, or we knock on a few doors to little effect. So we give up. Again. And feel guilty. Again.

Love and passion and enthusiasm are infectious. We see that everywhere. If you are doing something—playing a game, watching a movie, walking in the country—and someone says, "This is really boring," the whole atmosphere goes flat. But if someone is excited about it, then other people get excited. You will never attract people to Jesus if you are not excited about Jesus. Enthusiasm creates interest. Passion breeds passion.

Loving Jesus is also the antidote to legalism. If we give you rules and expectations, then your faith will quickly become formal, routine duty, and that will sap your energy. The joy of the Lord is our strength, Nehemiah 8:10 says, but there is no joy in just obeying rules. Enthusiasm for evangelism begins with an enthusiasm for Jesus. Our willingness to speak of Jesus arises from our delight in Jesus. Loving Jesus also counters perhaps our main impediment to evangelism, which is what the Bible calls the "fear of man," our desire for approval and our fear of rejection. A passion for Jesus means he matters more to us than other people. His opinion is the one that counts.

Loving Jesus is not a technique. Do not think about how you can communicate a passion for Jesus to others. Be passionate about him. Meditate on Jesus until he captures your heart afresh.

Love people. Step one in evangelism is being passionate about Jesus. Step two is being passionate about people—not just seeing them as evangelistic fodder or targets for gospel salvos, but as friends, people to love. Love will care for all their needs—physical, social, emotional—but gospel love also recognizes our greatest need, which is to know God through Christ. So true love will always want to introduce people to our greatest friend, Jesus.

As with loving Jesus, loving people is not a technique. We sometimes meet people who are excited about mission and community but do not love people. They love the *idea* of community, but they do not love the real people that make up community. They love discussing missiology, but they do not love the real people whom they encounter in mission. If you do not feel a love for people, then pray that God will melt your heart and give you love for specific people.

Love life. Third, we need to be people who love life. Christians should be the world's natural enthusiasts. We see the world as a theater of God's glory. We know it is marred by sin and scarred by suffering, but we also see in it many good things from God. We know that "since everything God created is good, we should not reject any of it but receive it with thanks" (1 Tim. 4:4 NLT). Sports, gardening, technology, literature, work, cars, food, fashion—all these things are good. All of them are gifts from God for our enjoyment. Our job is to have fun to the glory of God! Gardening may never become a major leisure activity for you, but when you meet an avid gardener you should be interested, enthusiastic, and excited by this person's joy in God's good world.

This attitude of enthusiasm reflects a robust doctrine of creation, but it is also a great way of connecting with people. Bill is an American friend of mine. He does not really get football (soccer), rugby, or cricket, but when he watches a game with us he is enthusiastic. He gets pleasure from our pleasure. It is the same with a hundred and one other topics. If Bill finds out you are interested in something, then the next time you meet you will find he has done some research. It is not a technique. It is not faked. He has a godly curiosity and delight in everything, and funny enough, people love having Bill around.

EVERYDAY MISSIONARIES

Jez moved to a new city a few months ago with a vision to plant a church. The last few months have been filled with speaking to churches, raising funds, designing a website, and producing a vision video. Our instinct tells us he will be a success. A couple of years down the line people will be asking him to speak on church planting because he will be seen as a "successful" church planter. When he launches the church, he will have musicians, sound equipment, a great venue—the full works. Jez is a good man with ability, character, and charisma. What he is doing is great.

The problem is that there are not many people around with his abilities or resources or charisma. Jez is playing to his strengths, and he is using his God-given gifting. But if that is what church planting requires, then we are not going to see many churches planted.

It is the same with the prevailing model of church planting. This involves a large church sending a group of thirty to fifty people, led by a fully supported minister. It is exciting when it happens, but if that is what church planting requires, then we are not going to see many churches planted.

The church is central to the saving purposes of God, and church planting is central to the mission of God. You have only to read the end of the story to realize this. Reverse engineering is the process of dismantling an object to see what it is for and how it works. Reverse engineering John's vision of the new Jerusalem at the climax of the Bible story allows us to see what the whole Bible story is for and how it works. Noting the way John's vision of the new creation becomes a vision of a garden-city in the shape of a temple, Greg Beale says, "The new creation and Jerusalem are none other than God's tabernacle . . . the true temple of God's special presence."[8] Revelation 21:3 says, "Behold, the tabernacle of God is with men, and he will dwell with them" (KJV). Paul Barnett comments, "Here is an astonishing teaching. The New Heaven and New Earth is the New Jerusalem, which is the Bride of Christ, both of which depict the gathered community of the redeemed ones. The new creation is the church, the church of the end time."[9] In Revelation 22 "the river of the water of life" flows from "the throne of God and of the Lamb" (v. 1). The word John uses to describe the tree that brings healing to the nations is not the normal word for tree but a word that refers to timber, which is used in the New Testament to refer to the cross (Acts 5:30; 10:39; 13:29; Gal. 3:13; 1 Pet. 2:24). It is the glory of the sacrificed Lamb, which illuminates the new creation (Rev. 21:23). So central to this climatic vision are the Redeemer and his redeemed people. This is the fulfillment of God's eternal plan "to bring all things in heaven and on earth together under one head, even Christ" (Eph. 1:10). This is where the story is going. In the meantime "God placed all things under his feet and appointed him to be head over everything for the church, which is his body, the fullness of him who fills everything in every way" (Eph. 1:22–23). God's ultimate purpose is not to see a solitary king ruling over ad hoc individuals, but a king with his people. Eternity is filled with the church.

So the church is at the center of God's purposes. The problem is that Jez's approach to church is beyond most Christians. At best most Christians fill rosters; at worst they are passive observers. Church becomes a performance in which most people are observers of the super-talented. The people of God are disenfranchised.

One of our ambitions is to take the idea of gospel ministry as the primary preserve of the professionals and give it back to the masses. Christianity has always been a populist movement. Stuart Murray says, "We know of few 'missionaries' in pre-Christendom. Mission depended primarily on the witness of unknown Christians—countless acts of kindness, family and friendship connections, provocative discipleship and significant conversations. Evangelism was a lifestyle, not a specialist activity."[10]

One of the key benefits of everyday mission is that it enfranchises each and every one of us. Everyday mission requires everyday missionaries rather than superheroes of the faith. We need to recapture the sense that gospel ministry is not something done by pastors with the support of ordinary Christians but something done by ordinary Christians with the support of pastors.

STEALTH CHURCH

In our culture Christianity is a bit like a bad dream, the details of which you cannot quite remember but which has left you with a sense of unease you want to be rid of. So we need to think about doing *church under the radar*. People are alert to religion in general and Christianity in particular. It is on their radar. They regard it as a threat, an intruder, something invasive they want to avoid. So instead of "opening a church" when we plant, perhaps we need to concentrate more on being the people of God, a group of disciples who take following Christ seriously. The term *Christianity* occurs zero times in the Bible. The term *Christian* occurs no more than three times. The term *disciple* is found over 260 times.

A lot of people follow what might be called "the Kinsella approach" to church planting. In the film *Field of Dreams* a farmer called Ray Kinsella (played by Kevin Costner) has a dream in which he is told to build a baseball diamond on his farm in an out-of-the-way part of Iowa. It is a crazy idea, but he becomes persuaded that he has to do it. Somehow it will be the making of his farm and save him from foreclosure. He clings to the belief that people will turn up to watch baseball—and pay for the privilege. In one conversation Terrance Mann, a reclusive author, says:

> Ray, people will come. They'll come to Iowa for reasons they can't even fathom. They'll turn up your driveway not knowing for sure why they're doing it. . . . They'll pass over the money without even thinking about it: for it is money they have and peace they lack. . . . The memories will be so thick they'll have to brush them away from their faces. People will come, Ray. The one constant through all the years, Ray, has been baseball. America has rolled by like an army of steamrollers. It has been erased like a blackboard, rebuilt and erased again. But baseball has marked the time. . . . People will come, Ray. People will most definitely come.

We naively think that Christianity is like baseball—the one constant through all the years. So all we need to do is open a building or run a meeting and "the people will come, the people will most definitely come!" But the *vast* majority are stubbornly staying away.

We cannot equate church with its meetings. The New Testament word we translate as "church" or "gathering" is *ecclesia*. It was the common term for any gathering, including political meetings (Acts 19:39) or even a riotous mob (Acts 19:32). This background causes some to argue in a reductionistic way that church only exists in the event of a gathering. But this makes passages like Acts 9:31 difficult to understand: "Then the church throughout Judea, Galilee and Samaria enjoyed a time of peace. It was strengthened; and encouraged by the Holy Spirit, it grew in numbers, living in the fear of the Lord." Here the term *church*, in the singular, is used to refer to what would have been multiple churches throughout a region of 5,000 square miles.

So the New Testament usage suggests a more developed application. It refers to *those whom the Lord has gathered to himself* rather than simply to *those who gather*. Paul is not merely talking about an act of gathering, for example, when he writes to Timothy about the appointment of elders. He draws a direct connection between the day-to-day managing of a household and the care of God's church (1 Tim. 3:5). This implies much more than organizing a meeting. Paul goes on to speak of "God's household, which is the church of the living God, the pillar and foundation of the truth" (v. 15). Like a human family, the church has a corporate identity and relationships that stretch beyond those times when they are physically together. None of this means the act of gathering is irrelevant. Regular meetings are important expressions of our identity and important occasions for building up the community, but church is so much more than meetings. Too often church leaders focus on the meeting because this is what they do and what they know how to do.

Our view of church matters because what we understand by church is going to be hugely influential in the task of planting. If we think church is primarily about the event of meeting, then the bulk of our effort will go into that event. We might be tempted to think that once that event is up and running, our job is more or less done. But if church is far more (though not less) than a meeting, then church planting is about the long haul of seeing authentic, alternative communities created that model the reign of Christ as they live the life of the gospel and speak the word of the gospel. George Hunsberger says:

> Churches are called to be bodies of people sent on a mission rather than the storefronts for vendors of religious services and goods. . . . We must surrender the self-conception of the church as a voluntary association of

individuals and live by the recognition that we are a communal body of Christ's followers, mutually committed and responsible to one another and to the mission Jesus set us upon at his resurrection.[11]

This is why we talk of church under the radar. People think they know what to expect when a new church opens, but when a group of people share their lives together as the people of God and get involved in blessing the city, then no one is putting up defenses. It is a stealth church.

MISSION BY BEING GOOD NEIGHBORS

Once upon a time a group of largely middle-class graduates in their mid-twenties moved into a deprived neighborhood. Three made the move first, and they were gradually joined by others. There are now ten in total, a combination of marrieds and singles, male and female. There is nothing remarkable about these people. None of them are hard-core or edgy. There is not a tattoo among them as far as we are aware. Initially the plan was to plant a church. A lot of time was invested in recruiting leaders, but to no avail. For some time this failure to plant a church was a cause of considerable frustration, animated conversation, and earnest prayer.

As this was going on, the Lord quietly got to work. How? Through these ordinary, unassuming individuals doing nothing more spectacular than being good neighbors. They were not a church (they attended a church elsewhere in the city). They did not hold meetings or do formal evangelism, nor did they significantly change the way they spoke or dressed. They just lived there—all very ordinary and unspectacular. Nothing they have done would merit mention in a missional church manual, but over a few years they have built credibility in the neighborhood through simply being the neighbors everyone would want to have. They do have a corporate identity: they are known as "the Christians." That is because they share their lives and are in and out of each other's homes. They sit out on the street in the summer and talk to people. They visit people in their homes, take dogs for walks, help with homework, and assist with gardening. They bake, they mend, and they iron clothes. They go to the local pub and as regulars have started a weekly quiz. This has led to helping a local couple get a cafe going, helping to organize a wedding for a local family, and contributing to various birthday parties.

It has been interesting to watch how local people have responded. From the beginning the Christians were marked out as different. The way they speak, the clothes they wear, and their education and life choices all make them stand out from the community. Single women in their late twenties and early thirties without children are unheard of in the area. At first there was misunderstanding. A degree of incomprehension remains, but the Christians are trusted, respected, and accepted. One day a block of houses opposite the home of some of these Christians was burned down—the culmination of a long period of tension—and it was to the house of the Christians that the neighborhood naturally congregated to discuss what to do. People have become Christians through their witness, and many others have heard the gospel.

The great thing about this story is that it enfranchises ordinary, run-of-the-mill, down-to-earth Christians. It opens up opportunities for gospel ministry to every church and every Christian. They are now a church, though the term is rarely used. It has turned out to be a case of church planting without trying!

Mission by being good neighbors, good workers, and good family members—that is what Peter calls us to. In particular Peter calls us to a distinctive attitude to others. We live in a culture where it is all about me: my rights, my pleasure, my fulfillment. God's people have an altogether different motto: "It's not about me; it's about God and others." That makes a profound difference when we enter the public square or the workplace or the home.

Peter's call to live good lives that commend the gospel is prefaced by a call to wage war against our sinful desires (1 Pet. 2:11). Our sinful desires are selfish desires, and Peter calls us away from self to serve others. This submission to others is not the end of self, but its true fulfillment. Peter's teaching is subtly but powerfully subversive. He calls us to submit, literally, "to every human creature." We submit to the king not because of his inherent authority but because he is an authority created by God. We honor the king, but it is God we fear. Likewise Peter instructs slaves and wives, when Greco-Roman ethical codes only addressed masters and husbands. Roman ethicists did not tell slaves to submit; they told masters to enforce submission. "This direct instruction to slaves and wives implies that both have a measure of moral responsibility and choice unprecedented in Greek thought."[12]

Yet from this radical position of freedom we offer submission: "Live as free men, but do not use your freedom as a cover-up for evil; live as servants of God" (1 Pet. 2:16). This beleaguered, ostracized, misunderstood Christian community is to respond by honoring everyone and treating everyone with respect. Our ethic is neither totalitarian nor individualistic, neither conformist nor fragmentary. It is freedom used to serve others in love (Gal. 5:13). As Paul puts it in 1 Corinthians 9:19, "Though I am free and belong to no man, I make myself a slave to everyone, to win as many as possible."

The film *Bobby* tells the story of Robert Kennedy's assassination in 1968. One scene involves a black chef named Edward Robinson (played by Laurence Fishburne). He is arguing with a Mexican waiter named Miguel as the staff eat a meal together in the kitchen. It is a time of racial tension, and Miguel is angry at the injustice and prejudice he faces every day. He cannot understand why the chef is so laid-back and compliant. The chef responds, "You know your problem, kid? You've got no poetry. You got no light. You got no one looking at you and saying, 'Man! Look at Miguel. I want some of what he got.'" Our life together as the people of God is a life of poetry and light created by the gospel. We are called to live a compelling shared life that makes others say, "Man! Look at those Christians. I want what they got!"

In a society all too often characterized by demeaning insults or belittling humor or scathing comments, the Christian community is to treat everyone with dignity. Imagine the impact this might have in politics, schools, and homes. Imagine the impact of honoring work colleagues, however unkind or incompetent or self-serving. George Hunsberger writes:

> Because we live in a plural world that no longer gives us privileged place and power, we have the choice to confine our business to the private realm of self and its leisure choices or to find new patterns for faithful public deeds. The calling to seek first the reign of God and God's justice means orienting our public deeds away from imposing our moral will onto the social fabric, and toward giving tangible experience of the reign of God that intrudes as an alternative to the public principles and loyalties.[13]

Peter calls us to a strategy of doing good: seeking to bless our neighborhoods, workplaces, and families. "I wish there were more people like you"—that is what someone said recently to a member of my gospel community. We are called to be the people everyone would love to have as their neighbors. How do we thrive as God's people on the margins of society? By living good and attractive lives. How do we impact the people who despise and ridicule us? By living good and attractive lives. How do we answer the charges of our critics and accusers? By living good and attractive lives. How do we commend Jesus to our friends, family, and neighbors? By living good and attractive lives. Everyday mission is living everyday lives in a distinctively good and attractive way.

We invest a lot in developing intellectual apologetic arguments and in developing people who can deploy these arguments. We do not despise this at all. It has an important role to play. But "it is God's will that by doing good you should silence the ignorant talk of foolish men" (1 Pet. 2:15). It is easy to get intimidated by the likes of Richard Dawkins, Stephen Hawking, Christopher Hitchens, or a colleague going on about the stupidity of Christians. How do you silence them? By doing good. "Faced by critics who want to carp and criticize? Don't answer back, just act: 'for it is God's will that by doing good you should silence the ignorant talk of foolish men' (1 Pet. 2:15). . . . The truly Christian way of winning a good reputation for the gospel is for the local church to begin thinking seriously about what practical good can be done in its local community."[14]

I (Tim) am on the board of a local community forum. Some of the board members can be quite vocal in their hostility toward Christianity. They are among the cultural despisers of the faith. But when they learn that I am part of our church, they have nothing but praise for what we are doing in the neighborhood. The interesting thing is that our church is small, and we do not run any big projects. But people see what Christians do. At the last meeting the chair was commending the work done by different people in our church: clearing up rubbish, contributing to the residents' association, working with local shopkeepers, helping refugees. Emily and Wendy are two teenage girls in my gospel community. Each week they help with a local toddler group by making tea, bringing cakes, and clearing up. You will not read about this sort of work in church planting manuals or mission textbooks, but people see it. Word gets back to me that unbelievers are impressed by what these teenage girls are doing. "For it is God's will that by doing good you should silence the ignorant talk of foolish men."

GOSPEL COMMUNITIES

First Peter 3:15 is one of the more frustrating verses of the Bible: "Always be prepared to give an answer to everyone who asks you to give the reason for the hope that you have." It promises so much, especially to those of us in the silent majority of introverted nonevangelists. We want to share the gospel, but many of us struggle to start gospel conversations. However, in this verse the focus is upon others to start the conversation as they ask us to explain our hope. Great!

The only problem is that this rarely happens. It is all too good to be true. What is at fault: Peter's expectations or our experience? A significant part of the problem is our failure to recognize the nature of pronouns. This is not a deficiency of grammar so much as a deficiency of culture. Those raised in a Western culture are almost bound to read the Bible individualistically because the culture is so aggressively individualistic. Every time we read "you," we assume it means "I." But Peter means "we," not simply because more than one person is being addressed, but because Peter is talking to his readers as a community. First Peter 3:15 is the culmination of a line of thought that begins with Peter saying: "Finally, all of you, live in harmony with one another; be sympathetic, love as brothers, be compassionate and humble" (v. 8). In contrast to a self-serving society, we are to live in harmony, and it is this harmonious life together that will provoke the questions of verse 15. As we have seen, the Old Testament descriptions of God's people that Peter alludes to in 2:9–10 evoke Israel's calling to witness to God through her corporate life. It is the good works of the church community and its life in the face of suffering that provoke questions about what we put our hope in and what we build identity around. It is through exposure to the community of grace that people start to see that followers of Jesus are energized by something altogether different.

This means that, although we can do mission on our own, it should not be our primary strategy. We need to do it as part of missional community or, as we call them in our context, a gospel community. A gospel community is a group of people with a shared life and a shared mission. They have a common identity with a commitment to pastoring one another with the gospel and working together to witness to Christ in their context.

A gospel community can be a church in its own right, or it can be part of a larger congregation. Moving to gospel communities may not require a big change of structure, but it does require a radical change of culture. A group of gospel communities that gather together on Sunday mornings may look like a church with house groups, but the reality is very different. The gospel community is the core unit, the place were evangelism, pastoral care, discipleship, and life take place.

Gospel communities are not like house groups, Bible study groups, pastoral groups, or ministry teams. House groups obviously vary hugely, and yours may function very much like a gospel community, but let us paint the contrast in black and white to highlight the change in the culture that is required.

House groups tend to be a weekly meeting. People talk about "house group night"—the evening in which they "do" house group by attending a meeting. A gospel community is a network of relationships that will probably have a regular meeting, but they are sharing life throughout the week.

House groups are often centered on a Bible study. In a gospel community the Bible is central, but the Bible is read, discussed, and lived throughout the week in the context of a shared life as well as through Bible studies.

House groups are often insular and focused on the mutual care of its members. Pastoral care is a feature of gospel communities, but gospel communities are groups with a strong sense of mission. They can articulate their vision for mission and identify the specific people they are trying to reach.

House groups are normally managed centrally by the church leadership, and leaders can be fearful of house groups becoming independent. Gospel communities have a mandate to reproduce organically.

MISSIONAL FOCUS

One of the common characteristics of gospel communities is that they have a missional focus or foci. They cannot reach everyone or contextualize to everyone, so they focus on reaching specific groups or communities. This helps the members of the community work together so that mission is a shared venture. These shared foci will usually emerge out of the passions of team members and the opportunities they encounter. The Holy Spirit is the great mission strategist.

We have found it helpful to make a distinction between proactive and reactive intentionality. As a team we may have agreed on a specific missional focus, but we still want to take other gospel opportunities as they arise. Our lives will naturally bring us into contact with people who are not part of our missional focus. Indeed we may have opportunities with people while traveling with whom we cannot continue a relationship or connect with our gospel community, but we will still live our lives as witnesses of Jesus and take opportunities to speak of him. This is reactive intentionality. We will be reactive to opportunities whenever and wherever they arise.

Where we can be proactive, we will pursue the missional focus of our gospel community. Where we can make decisions about how we use our time—where we shop, with whom we eat, and so on—we will make those choices in the light of our missional focus. This is proactive intentionality. Sometimes we can be proactive about the choice of our work and take a job that allows us to pursue our missional focus, but other people will not be able to do this. They will spend their work days being reactive to opportunities but then make choices about what they do in the evenings and on weekends to pursue the missional focus of their gospel community.

One form proactive intentionality can take is designating a time when the gospel community does mission or serves its neighborhood together. One of our gospel communities sets aside an evening each week to do mission together with the ethnic group they are trying to reach. They may invite people over for a film or visit people in local cafes. Another gospel community meets at 9:00 A.M. for a short time of prayer and then goes out in groups to hang out with or serve unbelievers. Some go to the park to play football, others host cooking sessions with young women, while others work in the garden of a neighbor. People are then invited back to a home for lunch together.

Our reactive intentionality means that new opportunities for mission can open up in unexpected ways. So the missional focus may shift from time to time. Your missional focus is not always something you can lock down, so identifying your missional focus will often be an ongoing discussion. Alan Hirsch suggests the following questions to ask periodically to help evaluate your missional focus:[15]

1) Are we in close proximity with those we feel called to?
2) Are we spending regular time with these people?
3) Are we too busy to develop meaningful relationships?

The important thing is to set a culture in which people understand your values and vision so that they are free to respond to the leading of the Holy Spirit. They do not need to refer to a plan or program.

Instead they are released to respond to opportunities as they emerge. The job of leaders is then to make sense of the chaos that results!

The following questionnaire is designed, using objective criteria, to give a snapshot of the health of a missional community. Do not use it as an occasion for discouragement or blame. Reflect on how you together as a community can take things forward rather than blaming other people.

1) How often do you have conversations with people in your missional community outside regular meetings?

   • *once a month*   • *once a week*   • *twice a week*   • *more than twice a week*

2) How often are people from your missional community in your home or you in theirs?

   • *once a month*   • *once a week*   • *twice a week*   • *more than twice a week*

3) How often do people in your missional community talk about how the Holy Spirit has been speaking to them through God's Word?

   • *once a month*   • *once a week*   • *twice a week*   • *more than twice a week*

4) How often do you talk with people in your missional community about your struggles to follow Jesus?

   • *once a month*   • *once a week*   • *twice a week*   • *more than twice a week*

5) How often do unbelievers spend time with your missional community?

   • *once a month*   • *once a week*   • *twice a week*   • *more than twice a week*

6) How often does your missional community spend time with unbelievers on their territory, in places where they feel comfortable?

   • *once a month*   • *once a week*   • *twice a week*   • *more than twice a week*

7) Are the prayers of your missional community gospel centered? Do you pray regularly for:

   • *one another's godliness*   • *gospel opportunities*   • *boldness to speak of Christ*
   • *the conversion of the lost*   • *the spread of the gospel around the world*

8) With how many unbelievers does your missional community have regular conversations about Jesus, and how many are involved in Bible studies?

   • *none*   • *one or two*   • *three or four*   • *many*

9) How many people in your missional community do your most significant unbelieving friends know by name?

   • *none*   • *one or two*   • *about half of them*   • *most of them*

10) Would you bring your closest unbelieving friends to a typical get-together of your missional community?

   • *no*   • *in theory I would, but in reality I don't*   • *only if it's specifically designed around them*   • *yes*

TURNING THE WORLD UPSIDE DOWN

When the apologists of the second and third centuries were defending Christianity, they pointed to the lives of the Christians as their strongest argument for giving Christians freedom. These men and women saw themselves as a third race, neither Jew nor Gentile. They lived as free men and women and used their freedom to do good. This is how the early church "turned the world upside down" (Acts 17:6 ESV).

Commenting on the dramatic growth of the church during the first centuries after Christ, Rodney Stark, the American social scientist, points out there was no great strategy, no leading personalities, and no mass communication.[16] Yet the gospel spread and churches sprung up all across the empire. By the middle of the second century Justinus said, "There is not a race of men on the earth among whom converts to the Christian faith cannot be found."[17] By the end of that century Tertullian could say, "We came on the scene only yesterday and already we fill all your institutions, your towns, walled cities, your fortresses . . . your senate and your forum."[18]

Alan Hirsch asks how the early Christians managed this rate of expansion when they were an illegal religion with no church buildings, no Bibles in the hands of ordinary believers, no professional leadership, no youth groups, no worship bands, no seminaries, and no commentaries—and they made it hard to join the church.

Perhaps some of these factors were not impediments to growth but assisted the spread of the gospel. The growth of churches was not restricted by buildings or clergy. This was a grassroots movement of ordinary men and women doing everyday church and everyday mission. The constant threat of persecution, suggests Hirsch, drove "the persecuted to live very close to their message—they simply cling to the gospel of Jesus and thus unlock its liberating power."[19]

Stark argues that Christianity grew because of the way it cared for people, both within the church and outside. He claims that two widespread epidemics during this period played a particularly significant role. The church could not clean up the streets; there were still dead bodies rotting in the sewer that ran down the middle of the road. But Christians cared for one another, leading to greater survival rates. This in turn led to an increased proportion of Christians in urban centers, which meant more people's lives intersected with networks of Christians at a time when traditional social bonds were disrupted by the epidemics. Christians also cared for non-Christians, bringing these unbelievers into the sphere of Christian influence and commending the faith to pagans. Stark also cites a number of pagan sources that complained about the good reputation Christians were gaining. Pagan priests fled for their lives while Christians were sustained by a more enduring hope. The church historian Henry Chadwick says:

> The practical application of charity was probably the most potent single cause of Christian success. The pagan comment "See how these Christians love each other" (reported by Tertullian) was not irony. Christian charity expressed itself in care for the poor, for widows and orphans, in visits to brethren in prison or condemned to death in labour in mines, and social action in time of calamity like famine, earthquake, pestilence, or war.[20]

Stark also draws attention to the distinctive way the church treated women. Most pagan girls were married off with little say before puberty. Christian women had plenty of say and tended to marry around eighteen. Aborting babies was also a huge killer of women in this period, but Christian women were spared this. Pagans routinely practiced infanticide. Archaeologists have discovered sewers clogged with the bones of newborn girls. Not only did Christians prohibit this, but they would rescue abandoned infants and bring them into their own families. Female infanticide and mortality during abortions meant men outnumbered women in the Roman Empire. Not so in the church. As a result, fertility rates among Christians were higher, which itself contributed to an increase in the proportion of Christians in the empire.

Christianity prospered in a culture in which people cared only for those in their own tribe. Popular entertainment involved watching people tortured and killed in the arena while crowds shouted, "Shake him! Jump up and down on him." In contrast, claims Stark, what Christianity gave to its converts was nothing less than their humanity.[21]

This is what Peter is talking about. In the face of persecution or the threat of persecution, ordinary Christians took the gospel the length and breadth of the Roman Empire.

It is not complicated. Of course, living differently by grace is never easy. God has not equipped us all to be big personalities with multiple gifts or oratory that draws the crowds. But through the death of Christ and the faithful work of the Spirit, he has empowered us all to live such good lives that others are drawn to Christ. However you *do* church, let it be nothing less than the people of God on mission together. In this way we are a city on a hill and a light to the world.

5

EVERYDAY EVANGELISM

1 PETER 3:15–16

"But in your hearts set apart Christ as Lord. Always be prepared to give an answer to everyone who asks you to give the reason for the hope that you have. But do this with gentleness and respect, keeping a clear conscience, so that those who speak maliciously against your good behavior in Christ may be ashamed of their slander" (1 Pet. 3:15–16). Some people are natural evangelists. They somehow always seem to get into gospel conversations. They go into a shop, sit on the bus, or stand in a line, and they end up talking about Jesus. We do not know how they do it. Indeed most of the time they do not really know how they do it. It just seems to happen.

Neither of us is like that. We wish we were, but we are not natural evangelists. We have to work out how to do it. So our best course is to make merit of our deficiency and work out some ideas for sharing the gospel that other people who are not natural evangelists can use.

How can we talk about Jesus in the context of everyday life? If church and mission are more than an event to which we invite people, if they are about ordinary life with gospel intentionality, how do we do everyday evangelism?

The first answer is to do everyday pastoral care. Think of your Christian friends as an opportunity to practice! If you find it hard to talk about Jesus with Christians, then how do you expect to talk about him with unbelievers? As you get more in the habit of talking about Jesus in the everyday with Christians, you may find it easier to talk about him with unbelievers. The links between everyday life and Jesus will become easier to spot. Let your unbelieving friends overhear you gospeling one another. We do not mean stage-managed conversations—people will see through that straight away. We mean exposing them to a community genuinely centered on Jesus. As people come into this community, they will hear the gospel being spoken around them.

We want to suggest some tools for talking about the gospel with your unbelieving friends. In many ways, the approaches are the same as those for everyday pastoral care, but this time unbelievers are in view. That is because in pastoral care and evangelism we have the same content and the same context: the content is the gospel and the context is everyday life.

EVANGELISM IN A POST-CHRISTIAN CULTURE

Many current evangelistic approaches assume a Christian culture, but, as we have seen, we live in an increasingly post-Christian culture. People are biblically illiterate. They do not start with the basics of a Christian worldview. Guilt, faith, sin, and God are all empty or confused concepts for them. They will not be converted through a ten-minute gospel presentation on the back of a napkin. They need a lot of nudging. They need a lot of gaps filled in, or else they will start with a deep-seated antipathy toward Christianity. They are not going to welcome a four-point gospel presentation, however well practiced.

If we could place people on a range of one to ten depending on their interest in the gospel, where one is no interest and ten is a decision to follow Christ, lots of evangelism assumes people are at around eight. We teach our gospel outlines. We teach answers to apologetic questions. We hold guest services. We put on evangelistic courses. We preach in the open air or knock on doors. All these are great things to do, but 70 percent of the population is at one or two.

Many of us know how to answer the question, What must I do to be saved? But we do not know how to *begin* a conversation about Jesus. Our only hope is a crass, awkward change of direction, like crunching the gears in your car. So you are watching football and you resort to saying things like, "At last a substitution. Did you know that Jesus could be your substitute?" "Great goal. What about you? What's the goal of your life?" "Come on referee! That was never a penalty! Did you know Jesus paid the penalty for our sin?" Here are a couple of implications.

First, we need to be patient and trust God's sovereignty. As often as not, our role is to move people one or two steps along the way rather than get them all the way to number ten in one go. God is in control of mission. He is sovereign in salvation. Trust him to take the little morsel of the gospel message you give to people and use it as part of his purposes in their life. "Make the most of every opportunity," says Paul in Colossians 4:5, not "Make opportunities." Our role is to live good and attractive lives under the lordship of Christ that provoke questions (1 Pet. 3:15–16).

Sometimes less is more. We often find when we are sharing the gospel alongside another Christian that we wish they would shut up more. They seem desperate to fill the silence. We need to give people time to think. We are asking them to believe a totally different worldview full of weird miraculous concepts. We are asking them to make a life-changing decision. Give them a chance to think before you unload another heap of strange ideas. Trust the Holy Spirit to work on their hearts. The Holy Spirit is the ultimate evangelist. He and he alone persuades people of the truth. He convicts of sin, righteousness, and judgment. He opens blind eyes. He melts hard hearts. And the wonderful thing about the Holy Spirit is that his pace is always right. While you are silent, the Holy Spirit is at work, and he will gently but surely accomplish God's purposes in a person's life.

When we get a gospel opportunity, we do not have to run through the full gospel presentation. At best that will be too much information. People will not get their heads round it in one go. At worst you may ensure they never ask you about anything "religious" for fear they get the twenty-minute gospel presentation again.

Second, we need to find ways of presenting the gospel at points one and two on our scale of interest in Christ and not just at points eight and nine.

We typically train people to answer the most frequently asked apologetic questions, things like, Why does God allow suffering? and What about other religions? The problem is that these lists of "top" questions are self-selecting. They are not actually people's most commonly asked questions. They exclude the real questions people ask, like, Where are my car keys? and What do you think about this dress? We cannot wait for people to ask the metaphysical questions. We need to identify gospel responses to the Where are my car keys? and What do you think about this dress? questions.

How can we do this? We want to suggest four points of intersection and four liberating truths that might help us use presenting issues as a window to the heart. This approach affirms much that people are already doing as well as brings some focus and edge.

1) FOUR POINTS OF INTERSECTION

We are all interpreters. God made us to make sense of life. So human beings are always looking to interpret life. We were made to live trusting in God's Word, for God's Word is the interpretation that brings wholeness and sanity to our lives. Of course, there are other interpreters and interpretations. Human rebellion began when Eve listened to another interpreter (Satan) and another interpretation (that God is a tyrant whose rule should be rejected).

Everyone is interpreting life. Take a five-minute snapshot of an office or someone's living room, and you will hear people trying to make sense of their own experiences. Plus we do it together. We are looking to one another for interpretation or for our interpretations to be confirmed. This is what the Bible calls "the world"—collective reinterpretations of life that shape us and to which we contribute.

Opportunities arise when a person's interpretation of life begins to break down. Any view of life not governed by God's Word is going to fail at some point. A problem or crisis in a friend's life is a moment of exposure. For example, if our interpretation of life is one of self-reliance, then cracks will appear when life becomes difficult or events overtake us. We begin to realize that we do not control our circumstances. Sickness, death, and disaster become a glaring reminder to us that relying on ourselves does not work.

If our interpretation of life is to look to others to satisfy us, then cracks appear when people let us down. Loneliness, disappointment, and resentment become a glaring reminder to us that relying on others does not work.

If we have interpreted life as a series of events in which we are to be satisfied, then the cracks appear when each fix begins to fail us. We become desperate for another drink, another relationship, another plate of food, another holiday. Our desires become more focused or our efforts more obsessive, and eventually the reality of our enslavement becomes public.

If we have interpreted life as striving to be perfect, then cracks will appear in those moments when we cannot sustain perfection. We start to cover our faults, lies creep in, and we hide from people whose opinions we value. We develop strategies to make us look more beautiful or clever or kind. We are trying to justify ourselves, but we cannot be justified by our works.

Sometimes people's interpretation of life breaks down when they find success. They achieve all that they ever hoped to achieve but then find it is not enough. They still feel empty, longing for more. We are made to know God, so a new spouse, a successful career, a beautiful home, or material prosperity all end up being poor substitutes.

Everyone Has a Gospel Story

The primary way we interpret life is through stories. *Everyone has a gospel story.* Everyone. Everyone has their version of salvation. They are gospel stories in that they purport to offer good news. In other words, there are secular gospels as well as religious gospels.

We can use the framework of creation, fall, redemption, and consummation or new creation as four points of intersection—four points at which people's stories intersect with the gospel story. Obviously people do not use the categories creation, fall, redemption, and consummation. But they will talk about who they are and what they are meant to be (creation). They will talk about what is wrong with them or what is wrong with the world—somebody or something will be blamed (fall). They will also have a sense of what needs to happen for things to be put right (redemption) and some sense of the state of affairs that they are hoping will give them meaning or satisfaction (consummation).

Creation	My identity
Fall	My problem
Redemption	My solution
Consummation	My hope

In Genesis 3 God's Word gets reinterpreted by the Serpent as follows:

Creation	You are meant to be gods.
Fall	You are held back by God and his insecurities.
Redemption	You can be set free by disobeying God.
Consummation	You will be gods.

Despite this rejection of God's Word and rule, in God's grace the Bible story becomes:

Creation	We are made in God's image to reflect his glory, to love God, and to love others.
Fall	We have rebelled against God's rule, but our self-rule leads to conflict, slavery, and judgment.
Redemption	God restores his rule by sending his Son and graciously enables us to live under his rule by paying the price of our judgment on the cross.
Consummation	God will recreate this broken world when Jesus returns.

There are actually lots of way you could tell this story. While there are clearly some wrong ways of telling the gospel story, you can define creation, fall, redemption, and consummation in a variety of biblical ways that will connect more or less directly to the people with whom you are talking.

Consider this snippet of conversation: "I'm leaving Jane because she's not prepared to see my point of view." It suggests the following gospel story:

Creation	I should be in control or sovereign.
Fall	Other people prevent me being sovereign.
Redemption	I will avoid people who challenge my sovereignty.
Consummation	My sovereignty is unchallenged.

This story is never going to offer good news, because it leads to broken relationships. The Bible's gospel story is:

Creation	We are made to find freedom under God's sovereignty.
Fall	We rejected God's sovereignty in favor of self-sovereignty (so this person's solution is actually the problem).
Redemption	God welcomes rebels back under his sovereignty through the cross.
Consummation	God will restore his liberating rule over the world.

Everyone is trying to find salvation. They might not ask, What must I do to be saved? But everyone has some sense of what it is that would make them fulfilled, satisfied, and accepted. Think about the people you know. Think about yourself.

1) How do they define salvation? How will they know they've arrived? *"I'll be happy, fulfilled, accepted if . . ."*
2) What must they do to be saved? What law or rules must they follow? *"To achieve this I've got to . . ."*

What these questions highlight is that some people (religious people) are pursuing a right understanding of salvation by the wrong means, trying to be reconciled with God through their good works. Other people are pursuing a wrong understanding of salvation. It might be marriage, a liberated homeland, success in business, the acceptance of friends, a happy family, a beautiful home, the admiration of men, the worship of women, a wonderful holiday, prosperity, or security. They might be pursuing their secular version of salvation through their own form of legalism. They, too, have a law to which they must conform to be successful or to find meaning, and their justification by works is no more successful than that of the religious legalist. On a good day they will feel proud of their achievements and look down on others. On a bad day they will be crushed. But because they are pursuing a wrong vision of redemption, even when they are successful they are left feeling empty and unfilled. As Tim Keller says, "Jesus is the only Lord who, if you receive him, will fulfill you completely, and, if you fail him, will forgive you eternally."[1]

Another window onto people's gospel story is their view of other people. Legalists routinely rank people, because they see life as a ladder that you climb toward redemption, and you assess how well you are doing in relation to the people above and below you. Those perceived as being above will epitomize their view of salvation and consummation. If they idolize wealthy people, then they may well see salvation as prosperity. If they idolize cool people, then they may see salvation as acceptance. The behavior they condemn will be the reverse of what they consider to be the means of redemption. So if they condemn idleness, then they may well see hard work as the means to salvation. If they condemn people who look uncool, then they may see following the latest fashions as the means of salvation. Here are questions to consider that help to reveal people's gospel story:

Creation:	What do they assume the world should be like?
	What kind of a person would they like to be?
	Who are their heroes?
	What would have to be in place for them to feel happy?
Fall:	How do they describe their struggles and battles?
	What do they feel is their most pressing problem?
	What do they feel they lack?
	Who or what do they think is responsible?
Redemption:	What do they think will make life better?
	What provides a sense of escape or release?
	Who or what will deliver their hopes?
	What are their functional saviors?
Consummation:	What are their hopes?
	What is the long-term project to which they are working?
	What are the dreams for which they make sacrifices?
	Have they given up so that their hope has shrunk simply to getting through the day?

People are throwing out their versions of the creation story or the fall or redemption or consummation *all the time*. Reflect on a recent conversation you have had with an unbeliever. Can you identify any comments in which he or she expressed alternative creation, fall, redemption, and consummation stories? How might you have used those moments to speak about the gospel story?

We are looking for points of intersection. As we begin to identify the creation, fall, redemption, consummation narratives of people's lives, we can begin to relate these to the Bible's gospel story. Sometimes you may challenge people's worldview, but look out as well for opportunities to affirm links between what they are saying and the Bible story. Most of the time we will not get the opportunity to do the full four episodes of the gospel story. On one occasion we might get them thinking about the true problem they face in life, while on another occasion we get the chance to highlight the way self-justification does not work.[2]

Case Study: The Slimmer's Gospel

Jonny Woodrow, one of our leaders in The Crowded House, has been attending a slimming program for a couple of years. He identifies "the slimmer's gospel" as follows:

Creation	I'm meant to be happy and valued.
Fall	I'm not physically attractive enough because I'm overweight.
Redemption	I can change through willpower, weight loss, and exercise.
Consummation	I hope that my body will be transformed, because then I'll be appreciated.

Along the way there are lots of signs of sanctification—clothing sizes, weekly weigh-ins. At meetings there are testimonies as participants bring in their now oversized clothes. You even sit around "the book" identifying righteous and unrighteous foods. At its simplest, the slimmer's gospel is, "I want to be accepted, and I can be accepted if I follow the rules." It is justification by works. It gives us an opportunity to speak of justification by grace. Jonny articulates the *gospel* slimmer's gospel as follows:

Creation	I'm meant to enjoy God and enjoy his good gifts.
Fall	I use God's gift of food to replace God and find myself enslaved by food and filled with shame.
Redemption	Jesus restores me by offering his body in my place, and he invited me to a meal with him.
Consummation	I can find lasting satisfaction in Jesus the bread of life, so I'm liberated from my need for refuge in food.

The following is a real conversation about food with labels added identifying how different statements reflect the four intersecting moments.

"It would be easier if we didn't have food" [*creation*].
> "Why do you say that?"
> "Well it just causes health problems and weight gain. I've never done well with it!" [*fall*].
> "What's your struggle with it?" [*fall*].
> "I like it too much! I've dieted on and off, but at my age it gets harder to lose weight" [*failed redemption*].
> "Have you always struggled with food?" [*fall*].
> "I guess I'm a comfort eater really" [*redemption*].
> "It's a bit of a refuge for you?" [*redemption*].
> "I get in from work and hit the chocolate" [*redemption*].
> "So you have a love-hate relationship with it. I don't think anyone has a real handle on how to relate to food. We're all mixed up about it" [*fall*].
> "Yeah, just look at celebrities. Always yo-yo dieting! All that money and they still can't be satisfied" [*failed redemption*].
> "Would you feel better about food if you could just get on top of your diet?" [*redemption*].
> "Yeah, but no one's on top of their diet" [*fall*].
> "No, I guess that's why there are so many makeover shows on TV. I think it's because we're not supposed to use food to feel better about life. It just doesn't work, does it?" [*failed redemption*].
> "No, I guess it's not worked for me at least" [*failed redemption*].
> "Food is a good thing, but we use it to hide. So it messes us up [*creation and fall*]. We get addicted to it and use it to control our lives [*redemption*]. The Bible says God made food as a good gift to be enjoyed. But the first woman turned to food to make herself feel like she was someone. Ever since then, we've turned to food instead of to God to get satisfied and make ourselves feel better about ourselves. But Jesus said he is bread from heaven! He's the one who truly satisfies" [*gospel*].

2) FOUR LIBERATING TRUTHS

Many people today do not feel a big sense of guilt. They have grown up in an irreligious culture. The guilt of falling short of God's law is not a feature of their thinking. There may be moments when they feel the need of forgiveness, but generally they do not have a strong sense of being sinners. They do, however, feel trapped. They do feel unable to be the people they want to be. And the Bible has a compelling and persuasive explanation for this—and good news of a way out.

According to the Bible, the source of all human behavior and emotions is the heart. In the Western world we think with our heads and feel with our hearts, but in the Bible the heart represents the totality of our inner selves. We think, feel, hope, desire, love, and fear with our hearts. All our actions flow from the heart. "Above all else, guard your heart, for it is the wellspring of life" (Prov. 4:23). It signifies our motivational core. Our lives, our words, our actions, and our emotions are all the outflow of what is going on in our hearts (Mark 7:20–23; Luke 6:43–45; Rom. 1:21–25; Eph. 4:17–24; James 4:1–10). Circumstances, upbringing, hormones, and our personal history all play a part in shaping our behavior, but the root problem is the sinful desires of the heart (James 1:13–15). Destructive behavior and negative emotions arise when we do not see God as the source of all that is good and so desire or worship other things in his place. A sinful desire is not just a desire for a bad thing. It can also be a desire for a good thing that has become bigger than God.

This unbelief and idolatry lead to slavery (John 8:34–36). The thing that our hearts treasure or worship will be what controls our lives (Matt. 6:21, 24). "A man is a slave to whatever has mastered him" (2 Pet. 2:19). The gods we create become our masters. People feel trapped in their negative behavior or emotions. They feel like they cannot change, and in one sense they cannot. Trying to change behavior alone does not work, because we are not free to change. We need God to set us free through the truth.

This offers a point of connection with people, a hook, an opportunity to engage. The gospel is good news of freedom from the enslavement to the addictive behavior and negative emotions created by sinful desires. Jesus says, "The truth will set you free" (John 8:31–34). Just as lies about God lead to the slavery to sin, so the truth about God leads to the freedom to serve (Gal. 5:1, 13). If I am enslaved by my worries, then freedom is found in trusting the sovereign care of my heavenly Father. If I am enslaved by the need to prove myself, then freedom is found in trusting that I am fully justified in God's sight through the atoning work of Christ. So behind every presenting issue are lies and desires that enslave, together with an opportunity to proclaim truth that liberates.

Because these lies and idolatrous desires create slavery in people's lives, when we proclaim the truth or when we call them to worship the living God, we are offering *good news*. We are not telling them off. We are offering liberation from slavery.

This approach engages with the specifics of people's lives. People are more likely to engage with the particular issues that affect them. People come with presenting issues: anger, bitterness, difficult parenting, shopping, addiction, economic need, depression, violence, and so on. We can do more than deal with these issues *as a context* for speaking the gospel. Instead we can treat these presenting issues as windows into heart issues. We need to connect the gospel with the specifics of people's lives rather than, or as well as, starting with big metaphysical questions.

This is not just addressing felt needs. It goes to the idolatries and beliefs of the heart. It takes you right where you want to go. Indeed a weakness of some approaches to evangelism is that they present ideas for intellectual assent. People can sign up to a set of ideas (they believe Jesus died for their sins and rose again), but the idolatrous desires of their heart remain untouched. Their motivational framework is unchanged, and true repentance has not taken place.

When we use presenting issues as a window to the heart, we are in effect contextualizing the gospel on a person-by-person basis. We identify the particular sinful desires that control people's lives and the particular truths that will set them free.

Case Study: The Rich Young Ruler in Luke 18

Imagine you are asked, "What must I do to have eternal life?" Would you ever dream of answering, "Spend your life serving the poor"? Most of us would regard such a response as suspect, even heretical. It smacks of salvation by works. Yet this is what Jesus says to a rich young man in Luke 18:18–25.

"What must I do to have eternal life?" This is a gift of a question. Surely the answer would be a model gospel outline. The response of Jesus does not look anything like "Two Ways To Live." Jesus does not draw a bridge diagram with the cross bridging the chasm between us and God. Instead Jesus commands this young man to give his money to the poor.

The reason is that this command goes right to the heart of this man's problem—the idolatrous desires of his heart. His desire for wealth and security controls him. A man who worships money is called to repent of his idolatry and express that repentance in concrete ways. This is just what happens a short time later. When Zacchaeus declares, "Look, Lord! Here and now I give half of my possessions to the poor, and if I have cheated anybody out of anything, I will pay back four times the amount," Jesus responds, "Today salvation has come to this house" (Luke 19:8–9).

Case Study: The Woman at the Well in John 4

Jesus promises the Samaritan woman at the well in John 4 living water that will truly satisfy. Then he asks her to fetch her husband. It looks like a tangent, but it leads straight to her heart. She says she has no husband to fetch. Jesus knows she has had five husbands, and the man she is with now is not her husband. This woman has been looking for meaning, satisfaction, and fulfillment in marriage, sex, and intimacy. But they are like water that leaves her thirsty again. No doubt there was real pleasure, but it did not last. It was not the real thing. It left her wanting more.

She tries to change the subject with her question about worship, but again Jesus uses it to go to the heart of the issue. The question is not *where* you worship but *what* you worship. She was trying to find satisfaction from a man instead of from God and in the process made an idol of sexual intimacy, but it could not satisfy. The math tells the story: five husbands plus another man. What are the patterns in people's lives? Are the words "If only . . ." a refrain?

Jesus, of course, has supernatural knowledge of her heart and her history. But we need not despair. We can get to know people as we share our lives with them. We can ask questions. We can ask for insight from the Holy Spirit. Plus, as with pastoral care, we do not have to get our analysis spot on before we speak the gospel.

In the case of this woman, the fact that she comes to the well at noon gives her away. You do not do the hard work of drawing water at the hottest time of day! But she does not want to draw water in the morning when the other women are around. She lives a life of shame. Her encounter with Jesus transforms that. After she has met Jesus we are told, "The woman went back to the town and said to the people, 'Come, see a man who told me everything I ever did. Could this be the Christ?'" (John 4:28–29). She goes to the people she has avoided with an invitation and an openness about herself. The shame and hiding are over. Jesus knew all that she had done and still offered her living water. That is freedom.

PROCLAIMING LIBERATING TRUTH

The four liberating truths that provided a framework for everyday pastoral care also provide a framework for everyday evangelism. They help identify the underlying unbelief and idolatry behind people's behavior as well as point to the truth that will set them free.

1) God is great, so we don't have to be in control.
2) God is glorious, so we don't have to fear others.
3) God is good, so we don't have to look elsewhere.
4) God is gracious, so we don't have to prove ourselves.

All of these truths are good news. As you talk with people, you can ask yourself which of these four truths they are failing to believe. Then you can begin to think about how you can speak that truth into their situation.

Consider, for example, people who are overly busy, stressed, and worn out. Consider how a failure to believe one or more of these four truths about God might be the root cause.

- They might be too busy because they are insecure and need to control life, when God is great and cares for us as a sovereign heavenly Father.
- They might be too busy because they fear other people and cannot say no, when God is glorious and his opinion is the one that matters.
- They might be too busy because they are filling their lives with activity in a desperate attempt to find satisfaction, when God is good and the true source of joy.
- They might be too busy because they are trying to prove themselves through their work, when God is gracious and justifies us freely through faith in the finished work of Christ.

PUTTING IT INTO PRACTICE

Identify Generative Themes

Generative themes is a term borrowed from the Brazilian education-alist Paulo Freire. Freire developed an approach to teaching literacy based on the issues that generated energy in a community. These issues mattered to people and so motivated their learning. Look for topics that generate energy in people, that make people excited, angry, agi-tated, and enthusiastic. These will often be windows into the things about which they care deeply.

Reinsert God into the Picture

Typically people leave God out of the picture when they talk about their lives, so deliberately reinsert God into what they are saying. Consider the phrase "I just can't say no to John." What interpretation of life does this phrase reveal? "My life has meaning and joy only when I have John's approval. John is the one who lights up my life. John is my light and my salvation. John has become an idol—a godlike figure who makes life full and complete." Now, what belief about God does that reveal? Insert God into the picture: "John matters more than God, or John gives more joy than God can give. I desire or worship or treasure John more than God."

Powerful Questions

As we have noted already, Jesus had supernatural knowledge that enabled him to see the idolatrous desires and enslaving beliefs of people's hearts. Most of the time we cannot do this (although sometimes the Spirit brings a special discernment). Instead we can ask questions.[3]

At a conversational level, a good question to ask is, *What do you want?* As someone explains a situation and perhaps seeks your advice, ask what he wants. What is his ideal outcome?

You can then ask, *Why? Why does it matter so much to you?* This begins to push beyond the outcomes he wants to the underlying idolatrous desires of his heart. The why question also helps you move beyond "surface idols" (such as a new car) to identify "deep idols" (such as respect) so it becomes clear which of the four liberating truths comes into play.[4]

Asking *What do you want?* and *Why?* is a simple approach that can create a platform to speak the four liberating truths as good news. "I just want the children to pick up their laundry," someone might say. Nothing wrong with that. But if this is generating energy and conflict, then maybe there is more to it. Push a bit further and it might become clear that she wants a part of her life under her control; she wants to be god in her home. The good news is that God is great, he is in control, and his control can be trusted.

Of course, repeatedly asking Why? Why? might make you sound like an annoying four-year-old, but you do not have to do it all in one go. You can explore these issues over successive conversations as opportunities arise. Remember that God is the great orchestrator of mission. We need not "close the deal" every time. The point when that is appropriate may come, and we may or may not be involved. We can trust God to organize the route.

Mission involves a multiplicity of activities such as sharing meals, helping with chores, hanging out, engaging in recreational activities, answering questions, offering snippets of gospel truth, and holding conversations that appear to go nowhere. Taken individually most of these may not look like mission. But if you persevere with prayer and gospel intentionality, then God uses them in his purposes.

Another helpful question is, *How's that working for you?* In other words, What are the results in your life of living for this [your functional god]? In times of crisis it will become clear that people's functional gods do not deliver.

Questions to Ask Yourself

In conversation with people, have in the mind the following questions. You may not ask them straight out, but they may direct your conversation.

- What do they believe (or not believe) about God?
- What do they want? What are their idolatrous desires?
- How do these idolatrous desires control their lives?
- Which of the four liberating truths is most relevant to their situation (the greatness, glory, grace, or goodness of God)?

ADAPTING TYPICAL MODES OF CONVERSATION

The ways people engage in conversation present many opportunities. We can adapt common modes of discourse. Let us highlight four modes of discourse that cry out for gospel responses.

Turning Confirmation into Reinterpretation

Often people are looking for their interpretations to be confirmed. They may make a statement in a manner that invites a response. Or they may pose it as a question. The little questions ("Isn't that right?") that pepper people's discourse are invitations to reinterpret what they are saying according to the gospel story.

Turning Advice into Proclamation

People look for advice. What would you do? Which of these do I look best in? This advice seeking is an opportunity to proclaim the gospel. If someone is asking you what shirt to wear, tell them to wear the blue one. We are not suggesting some weird twisting of the conversation ("You should clothe yourself with Jesus"). But people often ask advice about personal matters. The advice of others is most people's primary source of ideas and influence. When they face tough choices, they ask their friends. It is very easy to get drawn into giving advice, but this is often an opportunity to proclaim Christ.

"Should I go out with him?" someone might ask. "Why would you ask that question if you're not sure you love him? Is it because you need a boyfriend to feel complete? If you expect some guy to do that, then you're going to be disappointed."

Turning Complaint into Lament

One common form of discourse is moaning. "Whenever my friends get together we start by moaning to one another," someone told me recently. Christians can interpret this as ungodliness. Maybe it is. But maybe we can use the structures of moaning by associating it with the biblical category of lament. We declare what is wrong with the world. In terms of our four intersecting moments, these are all fall statements. We can perhaps also begin to declare gospel hope for that sinful world.

Turning Anecdote into Testimony

When people get together, they tend to tell stories—not big narratives or well-constructed tales but anecdotes. Stories that begin, "Do you know what my boss said to me today?" "I was downtown this morning . . ." "You'll never guess who I met on the way here." "The weirdest thing happened to me on vacation last year." This basic mode of conversation is a great opportunity to testify to God's work in our lives. We need to rediscover the power of testimony. By this we do not necessarily mean telling the story of how you became a Christian. That is a great thing to do, but that opportunity will be rare. What we mean is testifying to the power of the four liberating truths by relating how one of those truths has helped you in your life. This allows you to proclaim the truth in a nonconfrontational manner. Indeed people find it hard to refute another person's story.

It also allows you to speak of your own brokenness together with

God's redeeming grace in a way that disarms people's assumption that Christianity is legalism or that Christians think themselves morally superior. People might not ask, "Tell me how you became a Christian," but you will get opportunities to say, "I once faced a similar problem, and the thing that kept me going was knowing that my Father in heaven was looking after me." "Do you know what my boss said to me today? I had to tell myself God's opinion is what matters, not Mr. Smith's!"

Let us go back to the questions we highlighted as examples of the real, frequently asked questions of ordinary people. Where are my car keys? What do you think about this dress? Most of the time the appropriate answers will be "On the kitchen counter" and "You look great in it." But there may be moments when you can go further. You might ask, "Why do you always get so agitated when you lose your keys?" It could be because someone wants life to be under his control. The good news is that God is great. Or it could be she is afraid of being late because she fears other people's opinion. The good news is that God is glorious and his is the opinion that really matters. Or you might ask, "Why does looking good matter so much to you? How's that working for you with all your credit card debts?" It could be that someone sees salvation in terms of acceptance and the "law" by which he is trying to justify himself by looking cool. The good news is that God is gracious and we are accepted by grace through the finished work of Christ.

THE NEXT STEP

What is the next step? It is exposure to the Christian community. Here people will not only hear the gospel word but see it being loved and lived. They will see the power of the gospel to unite disparate people and make them family. They will also see us failing and falling out but then see grace in action. They will hear our message with a variety of voices and experiences. The different gifts God has given us work together to create a compelling testimony to the gospel. By exposure to the Christian community we mean, of course, more than attending a weekly meeting. We mean being introduced to the network of relationships that make up the church. We mean sharing in the life of the community in the context of everyday life. Often people dismiss our intellectual arguments, but they find it much harder to dismiss the compelling witness of the Christian community. "Live such good lives among the pagans that, though they accuse you of doing wrong, they may see your good deeds and glorify God on the day he visits us" (1 Pet. 2:12).

6

HOPE AT THE MARGINS

1 PETER 3:8-5:14

"Dear friends, do not be surprised at the painful trial you are suffering, as though something strange were happening to you. But rejoice that you participate in the sufferings of Christ, so that you may be overjoyed when his glory is revealed" (1 Pet. 4:12–13). Peter's readers certainly knew what it meant to live at the margins of society. Peter's letter is full of references to suffering, rejection, and persecution, but it is also full of references to hope. The perspective of Christian hope changes everything. It changes our attitudes to living on the margins, and it changes our attitudes to our time, money, and careers, freeing up resources for mission.

In all the contemporary talk of missional church and the plethora of cutting-edge strategies for reaching people with the gospel, not much attention has been given to the issue of persecution. It is easy to understand why. Many people are familiar with Tertullian's (c. AD 160–220) famous aphorism that "the blood of the martyrs is the seed of the church." But we are reluctant to take it too seriously. It is one of those sound bites that we are happy to recite but only because we are not in Northern Africa in the second century facing another onslaught from the Roman Empire.

Yet even a cursory look at church history should give us cause to pause. Consider two recent examples. In China the Cultural Revolution in 1966 to 1976 banned any expression of religious life. Believers were imprisoned and sometimes tortured. Bibles were destroyed, churches looted, and Christians subjected to humiliation. In the eighties thousands were again imprisoned. Yet there are now an estimated forty million Protestant Christians in China, perhaps many more. In Cambodia there were around ten thousand church members when the Khmer Rouge assumed control in 1975. Missionaries were forced to leave, and the persecution of the church was savage. Ninety percent of Christians and all Christian leaders were martyred or exiled. Hundreds of thousands of Cambodians fled to refugee camps in Thailand. Yet despite the Khmer Rouge's attempt to crush the church, it survived and grew. Today it is growing with around forty thousand believers and 750 churches. Peter Wagner once claimed that church planting is the most effective evangelistic strategy, but the evidence suggests we should perhaps modify this claim: persecution is the most effective evangelistic strategy.

So we end where we began: at the margins. Peter says: "Dear friends, do not be surprised at the painful trial you are suffering, as though something strange were happening to you" (1 Pet. 4:12). Painful trials are normal. We should expect suffering.

Peter says, "In this you greatly rejoice, though now for a little while you may have had to suffer grief in all kinds of trials" (1 Pet. 1:6). We rejoice greatly, not only in the face of trials but also in the midst of grief. What a strange and disconcerting paradox! In our culture, grief and joy are incompatible, but biblically they can coexist. Grief in response to our circumstances does not overcome joy, because circumstances do not threaten our inheritance. Tears cannot extinguish joy.

What is the source of this joy? Peter highlights a number of interconnected truths that feed this unusual response: the association with our Savior, the care of our Father, the support of our church family, and, most prominent of all, the hope of glory.

THE ASSOCIATION WITH THE SAVIOR

Peter stresses that the suffering he is talking about arises from our connection to Christ and from doing good in his name: "If you suffer as a Christian, do not be ashamed, but praise God that you bear that name" (1 Pet. 4:16; see also 2:18–21; 3:13–17; 4:14–15). But he is also doing something more than that. Peter repeatedly refers in his letter to the sufferings of Christ (1:11; 2:21, 23–24; 3:18; 4:1, 13; 5:1). As Christians we follow a Savior who suffered, so we must expect to suffer. Indeed our sufferings are a participation in the sufferings of Christ. Our ability to rejoice in sufferings derives from the fact that our sufferings confirm that we are united with Christ and so confirm that we will be united with him in glory. "Rejoice that you participate in the sufferings of Christ, so that you may be overjoyed when his glory is revealed" (4:13). Suffering is a participation in Christ.

THE CARE OF THE FATHER

Peter goes further. His readers "have had to suffer" (1 Pet. 1:6). In 3:17 he says suffering is "God's will." God is at work *in* our sufferings and *through* our sufferings. It is God who takes us through trials and suffering. If we remove God from our suffering, we are left with cruel, cold, impersonal suffering. But if we can recognize that our suffering is somehow in someway coming from God himself, then our grief, though real and painful, is not relentless or futile. God's ways may be unfathomable, but his character is not. We know him to be a good, wise, loving, and merciful God because he has shown himself to be that in the giving of his Son on the cross. That one act interprets all of God's other actions. That is the lens through which we should view life in all its complexity. Even when bad things happen, the gospel tells us that God is at work in them for our good and his glory. "So, then," concludes Peter, "those who suffer according to God's will should commit themselves to their faithful Creator and continue to do good" (4:19) just as Jesus himself did (2:23).

Peter, quoting Psalm 34, calls us to "turn from evil and do good" knowing that "the eyes of the Lord are on the righteous and his ears are attentive to their prayer" (1 Pet. 3:11–12). He concludes, "Who is going to harm you if you are eager to do good?" (3:13) The original Greek begins verse 13 with "And" and has the sense of, "And so, in the light of this care God shows to those who do good, who is going to harm you if you are eager to do good?" It is a promise of eschatological security, not necessarily immediate protection. Peter promises that our "gentleness and respect" will cause people to "be ashamed of their slander" (3:15–16). We look vulnerable and shamed, but we will be secure (3:13) and blessed (3:14). Our accusers look secure and blessed, but they will be judged (4:5) and shamed (3:16).

THE SUPPORT OF THE FAMILY

Peter ends his letter with a strange command, one we are often inclined to gloss over: "Greet one another with a kiss of love" (1 Pet. 5:14). It completes a series of calls, which are peppered throughout the letter, to love one another in the Christian family (1:23; 2:1, 17; 3:8; 4:8; 5:14). Often they come in the context of external pressure or slander (3:8–9). Above all, "love one another deeply," says Peter (1:22), after warning that our former friends will abuse us when we refuse to join them in sin. In a world that has made us unfamily, the church is our new family. It is easy for the world to ignore a solitary Christian living consistently as a believer; he or she can be dismissed as an eccentric. But when a diverse group of Christians lives for Christ as a community of love and demonstrable, mutual affection, then society will find it far harder to dismiss us.

THE HOPE OF GLORY

There is no doubt, however, that the dominant perspective in 1 Peter that enables us to face suffering with joy is the hope of glory. We can rejoice in suffering because of our hope of glory (1:6; 4:13).

This pattern of suffering followed by glory runs throughout the letter. Almost every paragraph contains references to suffering or submission and glory or hope. We rejoice in our hope of a future inheritance while we "suffer grief in all kinds of trials" (1 Pet. 1:3–6). The Scriptures point to this pattern of suffering followed by glory (1:10–12). Like Christ, Christians are rejected by men but precious to God (2:4–8). We can rejoice in present suffering because it confirms our participation in Christ's glory (4:12–13). Peter addresses elders as "a witness of Christ's sufferings and one who also will share in the glory to be revealed," promising that they "will receive the crown of glory that will never fade away" (5:1–4). Young men are to embrace humility so that God "may lift you up in due time" (5:5–6). According to Eugene Boring, 1 Peter is addressed to "those who are at the margins of society, reviled and accused. They know how they appear in society's eyes. They need a larger perspective, which the author provides not in psychological or sociological terms of self-esteem, but by helping them see their privileged place in the context of God's plan for history, a privilege they had not achieved but had been granted by God's grace."[1] Tertullian said, "The leg does not feel the chain if the mind is in heaven."[2]

Peter promises that, for Christians, suffering and slander lead to blessing and vindication (1 Pet. 3:10–17). We know this because it was the experience of Christ with whom we are now united by the Spirit: "He was put to death in the body but made alive by the Spirit" (v. 18). In other words, humanity judged and rejected Jesus, but the Spirit vindicated him by raising him from the dead. Jesus "has gone into heaven and is at God's right hand—with angels, authorities and powers in submission to him," which is the ultimate vindication (v. 22)!

We see the same pattern of marginalization followed by vindication in the story of Noah (1 Pet. 3:19–21). Long ago Jesus preached through Noah, but the people of the time disobeyed his message and wound up "in prison" while Noah was saved. Noah is a natural point of reference, because he is one of the supreme Old Testament examples of vindication. For years Noah built an ocean-going ship far from the sea. It is not hard to imagine the ridicule this provoked. All the time his warnings of judgment fell on deaf ears. Perhaps, like many of us today, he had days when he wondered what he was doing. We are not told, but ultimately he was vindicated. Those who ridiculed his message were judged, while Noah and his family were saved through water. Peter links this to our baptism. Every time we remember our baptism, we are reminded that we have died to this world and risen to the life of the coming age when we will be vindicated along with our Savior.

With this pattern of slander followed by vindication established, Peter calls us to be done with sin: "Therefore, since Christ suffered in his body, arm yourselves also with the same attitude, because he who has suffered in his body is done with sin" (1 Pet. 4:1). The willingness to suffer is a sign of our break with sin. We do not choose to suffer per se (3:13; 4:15), but we choose to break with sin even though we know this will lead to suffering. Peter anticipates intense peer pressure when we refuse to join in doing what we used to do before our conversion: "You have spent enough time in the past doing what pagans choose to do—living in debauchery, lust, drunkenness, orgies, carousing and detestable idolatry. They think it strange that you do not plunge with them into the same flood of dissipation, and they heap abuse on you" (4:3–4). Peter's message is clear: not sinning might lead to suffering, but it is better to suffer than to sin.

We suffer "in the body" (1 Pet. 4:1) just as Jesus suffered "in the body" (3:18; 4:1), knowing that we will be vindicated "in the spirit" (4:6) just as Jesus was. Meanwhile those who abuse us will be judged (4:5). Christians "who are now dead" appear to the world to have followed Christ in vain, but Peter says they are "judged according to men in regard to the body, but live according to God in regard to the spirit" (4:6).

At the end of the letter Peter gives his reason for writing. He has written "encouraging you and testifying that this is the true grace of God" (1 Pet. 5:12). What is this true grace of God? The preceding verses say: "The God of all grace, who called you to his eternal glory in Christ, after you have suffered a little while, will himself restore you and make you strong, firm and steadfast. To him be the power for ever and ever. Amen" (vv. 10–11). The true grace of God, the grace that makes him "the God of all grace," consists of this: he has called us to eternal glory after we have suffered a little while. Suffering followed by glory.[3] Rejection followed by honor (2:4–8). Slander followed by vindication. Peter has already described Christ's suffering followed by glory as "grace" in 1:10–11, 13, and said that suffering unjustly for Christ is commendable, literally "a grace" (2:19).

Peter needs to write to confirm that this is "the *true* grace of God," because there are *false* versions of grace that promise glory now or without suffering. To claim our nation as Christian and expect special privileges from the state is false grace. To claim we can leave behind sickness and trials and claim health and prosperity is false grace. To leave behind the struggles and humiliations of mission, and settle for the acclaim of the converted is false grace.

Peter says, "You know that your brothers throughout the world are undergoing the same kind of sufferings" (1 Pet. 5:9). Suffering is normal for Christians (Matt. 5:10–12; Mark 8:34–37; 2 Tim. 3:12). Many of us do not currently live in an environment of active persecution, but, like Peter's readers, we live in a culture hostile to our Christian faith. To an extent, because of the historical influence of Christianity upon Western democracy, we do not experience more suffering. Freedom of speech remains a cherished value. Perhaps we also avoid persecution by our passivity. We might talk about values or ideas in the abstract, but how often do we commend Christ as our Savior and Lord? The repeated prayer of the early church was that they might have the courage to proclaim the gospel boldly (Acts 4:29–31; Eph. 6:19–20; Col. 4:4–6). We, too, Peter tells us, should "not give way to fear" (3:6, 14).

Perhaps our lack of direct opposition should lead us to examine the nature and extent of our fidelity to the Savior. After all, Paul says "everyone who wants to live a godly life in Christ Jesus will be persecuted" (2 Tim. 3:12). The relationship between godliness and suffering is not a strict quid pro quo, but maybe there is an element of cause and effect. Peter calls us to set apart Christ as Lord and be done with sin (1 Pet. 3:15; 4:1). This will lead to two responses that, though contrasting, are sometimes combined: (1) malice, slander, and abuse (3:16; 4:4); and (2) questions and opportunities to talk about Jesus (3:15–16; see also 2:12, 15; 3:1–2). The challenge to us is this: when were you last asked to account for your hope? Are we living a life that makes no sense without the gospel? If we live out our relationship with Christ in a way that expresses itself in distinctive obedience to his lordship, then the world will either be drawn to that light or try to extinguish it.

RESOURCING EVERYDAY CHURCH

By definition a church on the margins will not have access to the resources of the mainstream, so how can we live well on the margins and how can we resource such an act of perpetual revolution? Most of the time it comes down to how we answer such mundane questions as, How can we do missional church when life is busy? How can we combine everyday mission with a full-time job? How can we find leaders when we are seeking to multiply groups across a city? How are we to be funded?

Peter's call to follow the way of the cross and embrace the pattern of suffering followed by glory provides the essential framework in which we must approach these issues. Once again it is hope that changes everything. Whether it is money, career, or the pressures of leadership, it is our "living hope" that is to determine our priorities. We thrive on the margins because we are men and women of the gospel with eternity burning in our hearts.

1) Material Generosity: Money in Eternal Perspective

There is a sense in which sin is contextual. One generation's temptation is different from that of a previous generation. This is part of the way in which "your enemy the devil prowls around like a roaring lion looking for someone to devour" (1 Pet. 5:8). We need to be alert, because the Devil changes his point of attack. Not many Christians living in New York today struggle with the temptation to bow before an image of Virachoca, the Inca god of creation. But idolatry is alive and well around Times Square even if it is not carved out of wood. We need to take a stand precisely in those areas in our culture where sin is at its most rampant.

One such area is our attitude to possessions. We live in a materialistic culture. Many believe the material world is all that exists; most believe it is all that matters. We treasure things that can be touched. Not only do they provide pleasure; they also give identity. This is how we make our mark in the world. Much of contemporary Western life is given over to the pursuit of possessions or security in wealth. Part of the explanation for this cultural obsession is the complete loss of a sense of eternity. If this life is all there is, then the acquisition of more makes sense.

The gospel makes a contradictory claim. Christians are a people of the future, the future that Christ has secured for us. "In his great mercy [God the Father] has given us new birth into a living hope through the resurrection of Jesus Christ from the dead" (1 Pet. 1:3). This does not mean that life here and now is irrelevant. It means life is to be lived in the light of eternity.

Jesus captures this perspective in his call not to "store up for your-selves treasures on earth, where moth and rust destroy, and where thieves break in and steal. But store up for yourselves treasures in heaven, where moth and rust do not destroy, and where thieves do not break in and steal" (Matt. 6:19–20). Or again, in this one-verse parable, "the kingdom of heaven is like treasure hidden in a field. When a man found it, he hid it again, and then in his joy went and sold all he had and bought that field" (Matt. 13:44). Advertisements promise meaning, identity, and fulfillment through possessions, but Jesus says true treasure is found in him. Jesus says, "Where your treasure is, there your heart will be also" (Matt. 6:21). Our attitude to wealth exposes our hearts. Your bank statement will reveal what really matters to you. Your credit card receipts reveal whom you truly serve.

Paul says that God "richly provides us with everything for our enjoyment" (1 Tim. 6:17), but then he addresses those who are rich, which in our world, where over one billion people live on less than a dollar a day, includes you! Echoing Jesus, Paul says, "Command them to do good, to be rich in good deeds, and to be generous and willing to share. In this way they will lay up treasure for themselves as a firm foundation for the coming age, so that they may take hold of the life that is truly life" (1 Tim. 6:18–19). Be rich not in terms of wealth but in good deeds. John Rockefeller was one of the richest men in history. After his death, someone asked his accountant, "How much money did he leave?" The accountant answered: "All of it!"

The goodness of creation means wealth is good and to be received with thankfulness, but the coming new creation relativizes the claims of wealth and liberates us to use it to bless others. John Calvin reflects this perspective when he condemns "ostentatious banquets, bodily apparel and domestic architecture"—what we would describe today as fancy dinner parties, the latest fashions, and home improvements. "All these things are defended under the pretext of Christian freedom," he says. "They say that these are things indifferent. I admit it, provided they are used indifferently. But when they are coveted too greedily, when they are proudly boasted of, when they are lavishly squandered, things that were of themselves otherwise lawful are certainly defiled by these vices." Wealth and possessions, says Calvin, are "good creations of God, permitted, indeed appointed, for men's use by God's providence. And we have never been forbidden to laugh, or to be filled, or to join new possessions to old or ancestral ones, or to delight in musical harmony, or to drink wine." But we can also "intoxicate mind and heart with present pleasures and be always panting after new ones—such are very far removed from a lawful use of God's gifts."[4]

We often talk of a "good church." When people move to a new area, we may commend a local church as a "good church," but what criteria do we use to make such an assessment? Preaching? Youth work? Music? For Peter a good church is characterized by love, compassion, forgiveness, generosity, service, and grace (1 Pet. 4:7–12). The preaching may be eloquent and biblical, but if that is the primary characteristic, then the church is merely a good preaching center. The music may be stirring and skilled, but if that is the primary characteristic, then the church is merely a good worship center. A good church is a church in which the believers share their lives together as an alternative and authentic society. Such a church will be well-resourced because no one holds what he has or who he is with a clenched fist. Just as a flower unfolds before the warmth and light of the sun, so our hands open as they are exposed to the grace of God in Christ. Grace produces grace, which is why a gospel community can only be a community of open-handed, undeserved generosity.

A good church is, therefore, a church in which the people "offer hospitality" not merely as a duty but "without grumbling" (1 Pet. 4:9). Cheerful hospitality will take place only when we know that nothing we have is our own. Everything we have has been given us so that others might be blessed. That is the point Peter makes in 4:10: "Each one should use whatever gift he has received to serve others, faithfully administering God's grace in its various forms." Believers are the God-given means of grace to one another as we love one another deeply, serve one another sacrificially, and honor one another humbly.

The key idea in 1 Peter 4:10 is that we are stewards or administrators; we faithfully "administer" God's grace. That is a radical concept. If I am a steward, then I own nothing. Everything I have is a gift, and it has been given to me to be a means of God blessing others. Consider the community created by the gospel through the Holy Spirit in the aftermath of Pentecost. We are told that "all the believers were one in heart and mind. No one claimed that any of his possessions was his own, but they shared everything they had" (Acts 4:32). This is the biblical doctrine of stewardship. We do not possess anything. Instead, what we have has been given by God to us so that we can use it to bless others.

Jeff Vanderstelt of Soma Communities, Tacoma, Washington, encourages his gospel communities to write down on a large sheet of paper all the ways in which God has blessed them: skills, time, and possessions (from houses down to socks). The impossibility of the task is part of its message. Once they have filled the paper, he asks, "Why has God blessed us with these things?" The answer, of course, is so that we might be a blessing to others in a way that brings God glory. The church does not lack resources, not when Christians view their possessions in the light of eternity.

I think of my own gospel community. There is a lovely freedom from possessions. DVDs, books, tools, and cars are all freely shared without hesitation. Time is likewise held lightly, so people are quick to help with repairs, gardens, chores, and child care. Not only is hospitality common, but people routinely bake extra food and take it to others to enjoy. I often find that cakes have mysteriously appeared in our kitchen. I know from my visits to other churches that this is common. Such attitudes can never be promulgated through legalism. This is a lifestyle that defies explanation apart from the liberating impact of the gospel, and it is this that gives these acts missional power.

Such an attitude to material things is both appealing and disconcerting to unbelievers. It is both invitation and threat. This is one way our churches are communities of both grace and judgment. The world is forced to a response. People may be attracted by this hope-filled lifestyle and begin to inquire about the reason for our hope (1 Pet. 3:15). Or they may be repelled by a lifestyle that exposes the emptiness of their materialism.

2) Relational Generosity: Time in Eternal Perspective

"Love covers over a multitude of sins," says Peter (1 Pet. 4:8). A key aspect of the marginalized Christian community must be its capacity for forgiveness, or what we might call "relational generosity."

There is an idea that being in community means we have the freedom to tell people if they have offended us in any way, but Peter says our primary responsibility is to love one another. That means that when others hurt us, we are not required to confront them. Why? Because love has covered it. Love does not minimize wrongdoing; it covers it, deals with it, and even in a sense pays for it. There are two popular ways that we deal with offense. We can confront the offender to get it off our chest, or we can hide it away in our consciousness and emotionally distance ourselves from the offender. Neither of these responses is appropriate. We love him strongly, deeply, passionately, and graciously enough to cover his sin.

People ask us how Christian community looks different from the kind of friendship enjoyed by others. The answer comes at the point of tension. Every community experiences relational tension; that is a fact of life. In a Spirit-filled, gospel community, that tension leads to the glory of God. "Love each other deeply, because love covers over a multitude of sins. . . . If anyone speaks, he should do it as one speaking the very words of God. If anyone serves, he should do it with the strength

God provides" (1 Pet. 4:8, 11). Most commentators assume this speaking and serving refer to the formal roles of preachers and deacons, but Peter is addressing everyone as members of this new society. He is telling us all to talk with a certain sense of weightiness. In other words, our words should build others up, bring the gospel to bear, and speak of Christ. Servant-heartedness is to characterize not only leaders but the whole church. The apostle is passionate about gospel living for everyone in the everyday. His focus is not so-called professionals or super-talented, but ordinary people living together by grace.

Living in missional community not only requires forgiveness, but also time. Relationships are time intensive. Everyday church fills every day, but it does not necessarily fill it with extra activities. It is about living ordinary life with gospel intentionality. It is about doing what we already do with other people and with a commitment to speak of Jesus, whether to encourage believers or evangelize unbelievers. Suppose you go for a walk with a family from church and one of their unbelieving friends. Or suppose you share a meal with a colleague and a single person from church. Or suppose you help someone with his garden and get chatting with the neighbors. Is this family time or leisure time or church time or mission time? The answer, of course, is all of them. This is what a member of my gospel community wrote in an e-mail:

> I have felt working full-time that I don't have much time to do the thing I love most which is spending time with people. I get home from work, eat some dinner, give my wife a kiss and then I only have two hours until bed and I am usually feeling tired. The easy thing to do is watch television, talk with my wife and then go to bed!
>
> I've had to learn that I do have time. We've decided we need to include people more and more into the mundane, everyday tasks that we do so we spend more time with our church and community. What that could look like is having people over for an ordinary dinner and let beans on toast be enough! Or taking the dog for a walk past a friend's house and stopping in for a cup of tea. Or, instead of watching television on our own, have others come hang out and watch it together. I was forgetting that this is what we are all about: just hanging out, doing nothing spectacular, but with gospel intentionality.

Still, many people struggle to find time even to share life with others, because their life is their work. If possessions can be a means of identity, so too can careers. In Western culture one of the first questions we ask when we meet someone is, What do you do? We answer the question with a job title.

Christians have every reason to value work. God himself is a worker. He has given us his creation to explore, maintain, order, and develop and with it a mandate for technology, art, culture, science, industry, and commerce. We are called to glorify God and bless others through work. But work is not our core identity.

Imagine a follower of Christ who is very able at her work. She is a rising star, not only in her company but in her profession. Imagine that woman choosing to maintain a forty-hour work week in which she is diligent and committed but refusing to work extra hours because of her commitment to her gospel community. How would her colleagues view her? How would her employers treat her? Extend that principle to a local church made up of people from various walks of life who have not been seduced by the accolades society gives to those who sell their soul to the company. We might find people who have chosen part-time work so they can help out in a local anti-drug project. Or people who have left a promising career so they can serve the disadvantaged. We might also find people who have continued to rise up the corporate ladder but without compromising their integrity, which is giving them unique opportunities to witness to Christ.

Such choices are possible because of eternity. In fact, such choices make sense only in the light of our eternal hope. This eternal perspective means that even if we should lose our job or be overlooked for promotion or abandoned by our boss, we live as those with hope and so commend Christ.[5]

In the end it comes back to identity. We build our lives around our identity, around how we see ourselves. If you see yourself first and foremost as a businessman or a housewife or a professional, then you will build your life around this with church as part of an orbiting fringe of activities. But if you see yourself first and foremost as a member of

God's missional people, then you will build your life around this identity. Jobs, houses, and incomes all still matter, but they are made to fit around your core identity.

Not only do you build your life around the community, but the community builds its life around you as a member of that community. So, for example, if together you decide that your work is your primary ministry, then others will support that pursuit. We have someone in our missional communities who has started an engineering business. At each stage of its development he has involved the community in his decision making. He has a strong vision for blessing others through his products and generating income for the kingdom of God. Starting a new business is demanding, but being part of a Christian community is not one-way traffic. The community shares his vision and supports his work. When his wife was unwell, people provided meals and child care over a period of several months to enable him to continue investing his time in his company. His business is not just his ministry; it is *our* ministry.

3) Leadership: Pressure in Eternal Perspective

Leadership is vital and necessary. Every group will have leaders, whether or not you appoint them. Someone will emerge who shapes the culture. So it is important to ensure you have in place leaders with the character described in 1 Timothy 3 and Titus 1, leaders who can set a gospel culture through their leadership, teaching, and example. To lead a gospel community you do not necessarily need to be able to deliver a forty-minute sermon, but you do need to be able to apply the gospel faithfully to people's lives. What counts most is not charisma or eloquence but godly character.

Leadership is vital and necessary in the context of a marginalized church. This is why Peter turns from talking about suffering to leadership in 1 Peter 5:1–4. He begins his appeal to leaders "So . . ." (v. 1 ESV), highlighting this connection. And he returns to the theme of suffering in verses 6–11. Moreover, he makes his appeal as "a witness of Christ's sufferings" (v. 1). Leaders have a crucial role to play when believers are under pressure. Shepherds are needed because the flock is harassed and in danger of being scattered. And once again it is hope that is to shape the attitude of leaders: "Be shepherds of God's flock. . . . And when the Chief Shepherd appears, you will receive the crown of glory that will never fade away" (1 Pet. 5:2, 4). How does this work out in practice?

Willingness rather than obligation. "Be shepherds of God's flock that is under your care," says Peter, "serving as overseers—not because you must, but because you are willing, as God wants you to be" (1 Pet. 5:2). There was a time when a young man had various career options open to him, one of which included "going into the church." Although a clerical position may not have offered the most attractive remuneration, it came with a number of perks—not least, impressive housing and social status. That would not have been the case among the churches to which Peter was writing. It is never the situation when the church is marginalized. "In some American and British churches Peter's exhortation would seem strange. Why should any elder serve unwillingly? The responsibility of church office has been trivialized; it is no more than a minor inconvenience that can readily be declined. But in countries where conversion to Christ is illegal and baptism brings a prison sentence, the office of the elder carries a different meaning. Quite apart from persecution, any real shepherd of Christ's flock will soon feel the weight of pastoral care."[6]

Enthusiasm rather than greed. Peter calls for leaders who are "not greedy for money, but eager to serve" (1 Pet. 5:2). We cannot litter our cities with communities of light if every gospel community must be led by a salaried leader who has studied at a residential Bible college. We need to raise up an army of leaders who, like Paul, earn money during the day and serve in the church in the evening (1 Thess. 2:9). We need leaders whose life choices are not determined by salaries and pensions, who take risks for the gospel and model reliance on God. Authentic leadership can be bi-vocational, and in a marginalized context this may be preferable. Unbelievers are often suspicious of professional clergy. They are more willing to listen to someone who works hard with integrity in a "normal" job. It also brings leaders into contact with people who would never attend a church service.

Example rather than dictatorship. Bi-vocational leadership also enables leaders to model what it means to live credibly in a context of suspicion and animosity. Peter says leaders should serve "not lording it over those entrusted to you, but being examples to the flock" (1 Pet. 5:3). The story is told of a guide showing a group of tourists around the countryside outside Jerusalem. He had told them how a shepherd always leads the sheep from the front and never drives the sheep from behind. As the bus was taking them back into the city, a tourist pointed out a flock of sheep being driven from behind by a man shouting and waving a stick. "I thought you said a shepherd would never do that?" said the disappointed tourist. The guide stopped the bus to find out what was happening. He came back with a smile on his face: "That's not the shepherd. It's the butcher!" Peter calls elders to lead from the front, to lead by example rather than driving from behind by command. Leaders should lead the way in mission. Yet in many churches leaders have fewer unbelieving friends than most people in the congregation. Leadership is not so much about developing a program that others follow as creating a culture in which others flourish.

Whether it is money, time, or leadership the key is hope, just as it was with our attitude to suffering. Those who lay up treasure in heaven are typically generous with the treasures of earth. Those who live for eternity are free to give time to mission. Leaders who live for "the crown of glory that will never fade away" (1 Pet. 5:4) serve willingly and eagerly (v. 2).

PRAYER AS A MISSIONARY ACTIVITY

How will we resource missional communities? Resources will come from a Christian community shaped by hope, but our ultimate resource is God himself. Peter concludes, "The God of all grace, who called you to his eternal glory in Christ, after you have suffered a little while, will himself restore you and make you strong, firm and steadfast" (1 Pet. 5:10). God himself supplies what we need. "Cast all your anxiety on him," says Peter, "because he cares for you" (v. 7). So prayer needs to be central to our mission strategy. Peter says, "The end of all things is near. Therefore be clear minded and self-controlled so that you can pray" (4:7).

This is a truth we all know in our heads, but our practice so often reflects an assumption that only our actions matter. So why do we not make prayer central? Perhaps because we think mission depends on us, or because we want to be in control. If we think we are central to gospel growth, then our activity will always seem more urgent than prayer. During a season in which some of us met for prayer at 9:00 A.M. three mornings a week, I would find myself back at my desk at 10:30 thinking, "Half the morning has gone and I've not done anything!" It revealed the extent to which I think my activity is what matters rather than God's. If we want to be in control, then we will restrict ourselves to situations in which we are comfortable. If my strategy is to persuade people with carefully constructed arguments, then I am in control (and if I am not, then I can read a book to acquire better arguments). But if I pray with an unbeliever for a specific need, then I am not in control of the outcome. This scary reliance on God is precisely what we want to cultivate.

This is a strategy that lets God be the primary agent of mission, that lets God be God. "If anyone speaks," says Peter, "he should do it as one speaking the very words of God. If anyone serves, he should do it with the strength God provides, so that in all things God may be praised through Jesus Christ" (1 Pet. 4:11). We speak with the words God provides and serve in the strength God provides so that God is praised rather than us. We put ourselves in situations in which we must rely on God. Peter echoes the sentiment of Paul: "My message and my preaching were not with wise and persuasive words, but with a demonstration of the Spirit's power, so that your faith might not rest on men's wisdom, but on God's power" (1 Cor. 2:4–5). "We have this treasure in jars of clay to show that this all-surpassing power is from God and not from us" (2 Cor. 4:7).

We need to view prayer as a missional activity. For us this involves three things. First, it involves routine, regular, organized prayer. In other words, we arrange to pray together because this is our primary missional activity. Second, it involves a reflex toward impromptu prayer. In other words, we try to make it common to pray whenever and wherever and with whomever as needs arise. Third, we offer prayer for unbelievers. When unbelievers talk of problems, we say things like, "Would you like me to pray with you?" or "I'll ask my church to pray about that." This allows us to ask people follow-up questions like, "We've been praying for you. What's the news?" This not only shows love for people, but it also shows that we have a living relationship with God. God is not simply an idea to be debated about which we have opinions. We heard, for example, that the son of a couple from a Muslim background was having nightmares. Someone promised that we would pray for him, which we did. A few days later we were told that the nightmares had stopped, and this created a conversation about the kindness and power of Jesus.

So we want to make prayer our central missional activity and our first recourse when needs or opportunities arise. Prayer is not a support activity to mission. It is itself a frontline missionary activity. Mission is never under our control. God is the great missionary.

QUESTIONS FOR GOSPEL COMMUNITIES

Below are some questions to help apply the truths we have been outlining. You can do this exercise on your own by asking whether the statements following each question are true of you as an individual and of your gospel community. Or you can do this exercise with a group and ask participants to identify those statements that are clearly true of your community and those that are clearly untrue. Celebrate what God is doing among you and identify what you could together do better.

A) God: Are You God-Centered?

1) People often extol the goodness and greatness of God in normal conversation.

2) Our corporate worship stirs people's affections for God (love, fear, hope, confidence, desire).

3) Prayer is a regular part of our life together.

4) People pray together outside meetings as and when issues arise.

5) When we pray as a community, most people contribute.

6) When we pray as a community, it is sometimes difficult to contribute because other people are quick to pray.

7) Our prayer requests focus on God and his glory rather than on us and our comfort.

8) We are trusting in God's sovereignty rather than trying to do his work of conversion or worrying about results.

B) Love: Are You Others-Centered?

1) People often see one another between scheduled meetings.

2) Most people eat with other members of the community at least twice a week.

3) People often help one another in practical ways such as doing chores.

4) People feel a sense of responsibility for one another.

5) People use the language of *we* rather than *you* ("We should . . ." rather than "You should . . .").

6) People are generous with their time, money, homes, and possessions.

7) People are willing to discuss their time and money.

8) People make decisions with regard to and in consultation with the community.

C) The Bible: Are You Word-Centered?

1) There is a hunger for God's Word and an excitement when it is taught.

2) People often talk about how the Holy Spirit is speaking to them through his Word.

3) The Word of God is often discussed outside scheduled Bible studies.

4) People meet up to read the Bible together.

5) There is evidence that the Word is changing individual lives.

6) There is evidence that the Word is changing the life of the community as a whole.

7) People speak the truth in love when others face pastoral issues.

8) People look to the truth about God rather than blaming their circumstances.

D) Grace: Are You Grace-Centered?

1) People are open about their sin and struggles rather than hiding or pretending.

2) Conflict is open rather than suppressed, and reconciliation is proactively pursued.

3) People repent of sinful attitudes such as anxiety, pride, complaining, fear of others, self-justification, bitterness, anger, and selfishness.

4) People repent of good works done for self-righteous motives.

5) People are not afraid to make mistakes.

6) People feel able to relax and enjoy leisure activities.

7) Broken people are attracted to our community.

8) We constantly return to the cross in our conversation, prayers, and praise.

E) Mission: Are You Mission-Centered?

1) Unbelievers are involved in the life of our community.

2) We often have opportunities to talk about Jesus.

3) We are flexible and take risks for the sake of the gospel.

4) We are crossing cultural boundaries.

5) We are contributing to neighborhood and city renewal.

6) We value involvement in work, business, art, culture, public service, and government.

7) We have a vision to start a new gospel community or congregation.

8) We are actively and generously involved in mission around the world.

CONCLUSION

NEXT STEPS

Christians today are marginalized, slandered, and mocked. As we have seen, the churches to which Peter wrote faced a similar situation, but Peter does not offer sympathy. He does not say, "I'm sorry to hear you're in a difficult situation. I hope you can make the best of it." Nor does he treat it as abnormal. He does not say, "I can't believe the way people talk about the Christian faith. It's outrageous. We need a campaign." The people of God have always experienced hostility. Jesus himself was marginalized and faced the ultimate rejection on the cross. This is the One whom we follow.

Despite our marginalization, Peter remains confident that we have something to offer our culture. We can still make an impact. Just as Jesus is the stone rejected by men whom God has made the capstone (1 Pet. 2:7), so rejected Christians are "a chosen people, a royal priesthood, a holy nation, a people belonging to God" (v. 9). "This is who you are," says Peter. "Not nobodies, not no-good neighbors whom everybody despises, but a chosen people, a royal priesthood, a holy nation."

Reading 1 Peter we get intoxicated with the idea of church again and again. It is almost as though the smell of what it means to be the people of God emanates from the letter. It is mind blowing and heart stirring. We love the concept of the church!

LET'S IMAGINE

We have, however, been around long enough to know that the reality rarely matches the rhetoric. Maybe you find yourself asking, Are we always going to have to settle for mediocrity? So the question we want to pose as we conclude is this: Do we have the imagination to be what we can and should be as the people of God? Do we have the desire to be the people of God together on mission? Can we move beyond church as a weekly service and become a community that shares life and mission? Can we be a people for whom church and mission are our identity rather than occasional events?

We think this is achievable. It may never perfectly match the biblical ideal, because the church is made up of people who, though saved by grace, continue to struggle with sin. The church is not ideal because we are not ideal, but some approximation is possible. God does not call us to mediocrity, nor does he call us to be a community on mission and then mock our failures. He gave his Son and sends his Spirit so we can be his people and live as his people. We should be able to take the reality of church life, place a biblical vision of church alongside it, and say, "Yes, I can see the resemblance. There may not be an exact fit, but they are recognizably similar."

So how can we put a vision for everyday church and everyday mission into practice?

We are often asked about how we do things within The Crowded House. We are normally reluctant to respond. We do not want to put ourselves forward as the answer. While we love our church and count it a huge privilege to be part of it, we are well aware of its failings; we do not have a structure that we regard as some kind of blueprint for others. We find people attributing a model to us, often wrongly. But we do not advocate a model of church. Instead we advocate principles that need to be adapted to each context. In fact, there are different structures within the wider The Crowded House family of churches, and we ourselves have often adjusted our pattern over the years.

Let us describe how we organize church life at the moment in The Crowded House Sheffield, where we both serve as elders. As we have said, we do so not to propose this in a prescriptive way but simply to encourage people to think creatively about how they might organize church life for everyday church and mission. Please do not regard it as a blueprint to copy but rather let it stimulate your imagination.

One final word of warning bears repeating: everyday church is not primarily about a structure but about a culture or ethos. You cannot organize people to do everyday church through structures and programs. People need to catch a vision and learn how to live that out day by day. Structures can help or hinder, but they cannot generate a communal identity or a missional lifestyle. Primarily everyday church needs to be taught and modeled. It is about culture change.

A GATHERING OF GOSPEL COMMUNITIES

We currently have a number of gospel communities scattered across the city. They are the heart of church life. They are church at street level. This is where community, mission, pastoral care, prayer, baptism, Communion, and the application of God's Word take place. This is where people share life and mission.

Once a week the gospel communities come together for what we call a "gathering." The gospel communities are the primary focus for church life, but the gathering is also an expression of church. It represents the people of God assembled together under the Word of God. So, although the primary place of belonging is the gospel community, the weekly event is also important. This is where we stir our minds and our hearts to action through singing God's praises together, sharing stories to inspire one another, and learning from the Word. For us, this is where the main Bible teaching normally takes place. Here we set the vision and culture for our gospel communities. This allows the gospel communities to focus their energies on community and mission. They are also encouraged to apply what has been taught in the gathering to the specifics of their lives and their life together.

But our gathering is just a couple of hours a week. It is in our gospel communities that church happens day by day. This is the context in which we are in and out of each others' lives and homes, sharing meals, resources, problems, joys, sorrows, and opportunities. Sharing life. In our gospel communities we are being the people of God together on mission. So we describe our gospel communities as churches and speak of our gathering as a gathering *of* gospel communities rather than a gathering *with* gospel communities.

In any context the weekly gathering is going to be important for setting a gospel culture and a missional vision, but it cannot achieve all that the New Testament envisions for church life. It cannot be a context for the one anothering of the New Testament. Moreover, if it is seen as primary, then all these other things are viewed as secondary. If the bulk of a church's time and energy goes into the Sunday meeting, then everyday church will not happen.

Doing church as a large gathering is the easy option. You can be friends with anyone when all that's required is meeting for a couple of hours on a Sunday morning. You spend most of that time singing and listening to someone else talking. In a gospel community you are forced to rub shoulders with people day to day. People let you down and disappoint you. People say things about you or do not do things they said they will do. That is when it is hard to love and serve and forgive, but it is precisely in the everyday that we are called to be the people of God. If we are not the people of God in these moments, we cannot claim to be the people of God on a Sunday morning.

We often find ourselves accused of being against big church. It is not true. We do not care what size your gathering is. Our focus is not on what happens on a Sunday morning. Our concern is what happens during the rest of the week. Our cutting edge is not our Sunday event but gospel communities living lives together on mission out there at street level. What we do in our gathering is designed to facilitate and sharpen that everyday life of the church, so it is wrong to say we do not like big church. We do not like big events that distract from the everyday, that pull resources away from the everyday, that switch the focus from everyday church to a weekly performance.

We also find ourselves accused of being against monologue preaching. Again, it is not true. Our gatherings typically involve a sermon. What we question is the privileged status of the monologue. It is a good way to teach the Bible, but it is not the only way or a necessary way. The Bible itself describes the Word being taught through a variety of methods without privileging one above another. What matters is that the Word is central to our lives and our life together. We want to equip and liberate people to proclaim the Bible to one another throughout the week. We want the Word, as it were, pushed down into everyday life.

The gospel community is much more than a meeting. It is not an event but an identity, a community of God's people doing mission together. The gathering, too, is more than a meeting. It is the network of gospel communities working together to reach the city. The gathering of gospel communities has a shared leadership, which better enables us to cooperate. It also means we can put younger leaders in place within a supportive structure and create gospel communities on the fly in response to evangelistic opportunities. This collective identity with a collective meeting means the church is more reproducible. We do not need a lot in place to start a new gospel community, because leaders are supported by a wider network, and good Bible teaching is assured through the gathering. So gospel communities can be light, flexible, and adaptable. They can even be expendable in the sense that we can innovate and take risks without fear of failure.

The gospel communities can also be encouraged to adapt their activities, location, style, and so on to the people they are trying to reach. They are free to be very contextual expressions of church, perhaps with a focus on a specific ethnic or social group, because the gathering gives full expression to the unity we have in Christ, which transcends cultural differences. We want to express both the particularity of the gospel (through contextual gospel communities) and the universality of the gospel (through the unity of the gathering).

TRANSITIONING TO EVERYDAY CHURCH

How can you transition a church to one in which the focus is on everyday church and mission?

If you are a large church, then our advice is not to change all your structures but to create a working model. In other words, say to a handful of people, "Go, do it." Teach them, train them, lead them, and show them, and then release them to be a gospel community within your church. Then encourage this group to talk to other people about how it is going—their vision, their joys, their frustrations. In this way the people of your church have the chance to observe a gospel community in action. Then, as you teach about how the gospel gives us a communal and missional identity, you can point to what is happening and say this is what it looks like. As people hear what is happening, it may spark their imagination, and they too may start to catch the vision.

You may then want to take your home groups or small groups and release them to be gospel communities. Give them a mandate to be church and to do mission and to reproduce. Rather than dismantle church life, you can gradually shift the focus to everyday church. Make the gospel communities the front door and the gathering the support structure rather than the other way around. Or keep a big lighthouse model of church with its beam of light sweeping across the whole city but at the same time get that light dispersed at street level through the gospel communities.

If you are a small church, then be a gospel community. Stop worrying about putting on events and programs that mirror big churches. Instead, start being the people of God together on mission. Hang out together throughout the week. Get in and out of each other's homes. Let people know the struggles you are facing and the opportunities you have. Find ways in which your lives can intersect with one another. Invite unbelievers to be part of this community life.

When we first started doing gospel community, we acted as though we were a big church. We tried to compress a large gathering into someone's front room. It was embarrassing. I even spoke from a lectern. With a small gathering you have the opportunity to be relaxed and informal and just to be God's people together without any paraphernalia. When you outgrow a front room, you can think about creating two gospel communities and perhaps coming together in a slightly larger venue on a regular basis for a gathering.

WHAT STOPS YOU FROM DOING EVERYDAY CHURCH?

Let us suggest five obstacles that encourage people to maintain existing structures, even when they inhibit them from being the people of God together on mission.

1) The first obstacle is one we touched on in chapter 2: the endemic individualism of our culture that also pervades our attitudes as Christians. Our culture has made a virtue of an integral part of our fallenness: our desire to control our own lives. This is the air we breathe. I assume the right to live my life as if it is all about me and the right to make decisions for myself without reference to others. We cannot be the people of God with a communal and missional identity without opening up our lives to one another and allowing our decisions to be shaped by the community to which we belong.

2) A second obstacle is pride. We prize self-sufficiency. "I did it on my own," we say, not with shame but with pride. "I did it my way." But the biblical picture of church says we need to live in community because the Christian life is a communal life. We need one another. I need you, and you need me.

3) A third obstacle is our desire for comfort. We do not want to open our lives and homes to people. People we like are okay, but everyday church puts all sorts of people in our path and on our sofa. We do not move out of our comfort zones.

4) Fourth, fear is an obstacle, the fear that people might see us for who we really are, up close and personal. We can appear a great Christian in the pulpit or in the pew each Sunday, but we cannot appear a great Christian when people see us lose our temper with our children or answer our spouse sharply.

5) Obstacle number five is people. Libraries, they say, would be wonderful places to run if it were not for people wanting to borrow books. Many people have the same attitude toward missional church. They are inspired by the theory of community and mission. They read all the books and endlessly lecture their friends. They love the church in the abstract. It is people with whom they have a problem, so they are dismissive of actual churches. None matches their ideals. If only there was a way to do community without people! People, it is true, are a problem. When you start sharing everyday life, you see one another's issues. My

brothers and sisters are *my* problem just as *I* am their problem, and just
as I am to be a means of grace to them, so they will be a means of grace
to me.

So what are the solutions? The first solution is the gospel. The
people of God living life together on mission *is the good life*. This is
life as it was meant to be lived. We see this in creation: we are made
for community with God and others and to image God's glory in his
world. We see this in Abraham and Israel: at the heart of God's purposes are not isolated individuals but a people whose life is to draw
the nations to God. We see this in Jesus: he is the true Israel, the true
people of God, and the light of the world who calls his disciples to be
his new community and to be a city on a hill that cannot be hidden.
We see this in the new creation: God dwells among his people and
makes them his own. God's purpose has always been to have a people
who are his people through whom he reveals his glory in the world.
This is how God defines the good life: the people of God together in
community making known the glory of God. This is the gospel. This
is why Jesus died. Jesus did not die to save isolated individuals. He
died for his church. He died and rose and sent the Spirit to create a
people who would be his people and through whom he would reveal
his glory. Because it is the gospel that is solution number one, there is
no solution number two. If you want to keep a professional view of
church with a detached life from other believers, you do not understand the gospel.

Everyday church will expose our idols. You never really know
what drives you until you live in community. Other people threaten or
thwart our sinful desires. Suddenly our idols keep popping up all over
the place. They sit on the mantelpiece of our heart until somebody
knocks them off. Then we cry out in protest or dive to catch them. But
let them fall! The pain of having our idols smashed only serves to point
us to the one true Lord.

Either everyday church will witness to God's grace in our lives or
it will fracture. We cannot "achieve" everyday church. It grows out of
God's grace to us and to others. It is the fruit of grace and therefore

a testimony to grace. When people see us living life together—loving, serving, forgiving, forbearing, supporting, encouraging, and proclaiming the gospel to one another—it will provoke questions.

> Finally, all of you, live in harmony with one another; be sympathetic, love as brothers, be compassionate and humble. . . . In your hearts set apart Christ as Lord. Always be prepared to give an answer to everyone who asks you to give the reason for the hope that you have. But do this with gentleness and respect. (1 Pet. 3:8, 15)

NOTES

Introduction

1. Tim Chester and Steve Timmis, *Total Church: A Radical Reshaping Around Gospel and Community* (Nottingham: Inter-Varsity, 2007; Wheaton, IL: Crossway, 2009).

Chapter 1: Life at the Margins

1. The Barna Group, "Un-churched Population Nears 100 Million in the U.S.," barna.org, 19 March 2007, http://www.barna.org/barna-update/article/12-faithspirituality/107-un-churched-population-nears-100-million-in-the-us.

2. "The Decline and Fall of Christian America," *Newsweek*, April 13, 2009.

3. Scott Thomas, "This Is Why We Plant Churches," Mars Hill Blog, October 21, 2010, http://blog.marshillchurch.org/2010/10/21/this-is-why-we-plant-churches; and D. J. Chuang, "Churches Closing and Pastors Leaving," http://djchuang.com, 31 January 2010, djchuang.com/2010/churches-closing-and-pastors-leaving.

4. Cited in Eddie Gibbs, *Church Next: Quantum Changes in Christian Ministry* (Nottingham: Inter-Varsity, 2000), 15.

5. Peter Berger, "Secularization Falsified," *First Things*, February 2008, http://www.firstthings.com/article/2008/01/002-secularization-falsified-1; see also Peter Berger, Effie Fokas, and Grace Davie, *Religious America, Secular Europe?* (Aldershot: Ashgate, 2008), emphasis original.

6. Ibid.

7. The Barna Group, "New Statistics on Church Attendance and Avoidance," barna.org, 3 March 2008, http://www.barna.org/barna-update/article/18-congregations/45-new-statistics-on-church-attendance-and-avoidance.

8. The statistical picture is muddied by differing definitions and methodologies. Americans often use *unchurched* to refer to people who do not attend church regularly rather than to people who never have any contact with a church.

9. Forty-two percent of people in the Northwest are unchurched (or de-churched) and 39 percent in the Northeast, according to the Barna research.

10. Barna, "New Statistics on Church Attendance and Avoidance."

11. See Jacinta Ashworth and Ian Farthing, "Churchgoing in the UK" (London: Tearfund, 2007). The Tearfund Report and the UK Government's British

Social Attitudes surveys asked about "typical" church attendance across the UK and produced figures of 10 percent and 9.5 percent, respectively.

12. The English Church Census is based on a snapshot of a particular week, and it suggests 6.1 percent of the population of England attends church. Evangelical Alliance UK, "2005 Church Census," eauk.org, November 2006, http://www.eauk.org/resources/info/statistics/2005englishchurchcensus.cfm.

13. Ibid.

14. Maria Mackay, "Researcher Anticipates Further Church Decline in 2010s," *Christian Today*, May 22, 2010, http://www.christiantoday.com/article/researcher.anticipates.further.church.decline.in.2010s/25949.htm.

15. Philip Richter and Leslie Francis, *Gone but Not Forgotten* (London: Darton, Longman & Todd, 1998).

16. *Mission-Shaped Church: Church Planting and Fresh Expressions of Church in a Changing Context* (London: Church House, 2004), 36–39.

17. Ashworth and Farthing, "Churchgoing in the UK," 7, 24. This report found that a third of UK adults are dechurched and a third are nonchurched, but these proportions exclude adherents of other religions. The report found that 15 percent of UK adults attend church at least once a month with a further 10 percent fringe who attend at least once a year. Of the remaining 75 percent, 6 percent claim they might attend at some point in the future. This leaves almost 70 percent with no intention of ever attending a church service.

18. Ibid., 25.

19. Ibid., 18.

20. Jim Petersen, *Church without Walls: Moving beyond Traditional Boundaries* (Colorado Springs, CO: NavPress, 1992), 110–11.

21. Cited in "European Christian Demographics," Greater Europe Mission, http://www.joshuaproject.net/assets/unreachedeurope.pdf. The least responsive "mega-peoples" are Swedish, Russian, Lithuanian, Polish, Georgian, Serb, French, Irish, Czech, and Italian.

22. Ibid.

23. John Bellamy and Keith Castle, *2001 Church Attendance Estimates*, National Church Life Survey, Occasional Paper 3 (2004), 11, http://www.ncls.org.au/download/doc2270/NCLSOccasionalPaper3.pdf; and Jason Mandryk, *Operation World*, 7th ed. (Colorado Springs, CO: Biblica, 2010).

24. Ruth Powell and Kathy Jacka, *Moving beyond Forty Years of Missing Generations*, National Church Life Survey, Occasional Paper 10 (2008), 6.

25. Rob Spink, "Work Culture," *spinkingoutloud*, July 25, 2010, http://spinkingoutloud.wordpress.com/2010/07/25/work-culture.

26. George G. Hunter, *How to Reach Secular People* (Nashville, TN: Abingdon, 1992), 24.

27. Lyndon Bowring, "At the Heart of CARE," *CARE Today* 20 (Autumn 2010): 4.

28. Stuart Murray, *Post-Christendom: Church and Mission in a Strange New World* (Carlisle: Paternoster, 2004), 11–12.

29. Philip Jenkins, *The Next Christendom: The Coming of Global Christianity* (New York: Oxford University Press), 2002.

30. Cited in Ashworth and Farthing, "Churchgoing in the UK," 7.

31. Cited in Matthew Hughes, ed., *Social Trends*, 40th ed. (Basingstoke: Office for National Statistics, Palgrave Macmillan, 2010), 197–98.

32. Nick Spencer and Graham Tomlin, *The Responsive Church: Listening to Our World, Listening to God* (Nottingham: Inter-Varsity, 2005), 27–31.

33. *Mission-Shaped Church*, 11.

34. Stuart Murray, "Christendom and Post-Christendom," Missional Church Network, http://www.missionalchurchnetwork.com/wp-content/uploads/2010/04/christendom-murray.pdf, 17.

35. The Church of England, "Provisional Attendance Figures for 2008 Released," Church of England Readers, January 22, 2010, http://www.cofe.anglican.org/news/pr1310.html.

36. *Mission-Shaped Church*, 11.

37. John Finney, *Finding Faith Today: How Does It Happen?* (London: British and Foreign Bible Society, 1992), 57.

38. Murray, *Post-Christendom*, 234.

39. See Tim Chester, *Good News to the Poor* (Nottingham: Inter-Varsity, 2004).

40. Finney, *Finding Faith Today*.

41. Hazel Southam, "Church Predicts Death of Sunday School," *The Independent*, July 30, 2000, http://www.independent.co.uk/news/uk/this-britain/church-predicts-death-of-sunday-school-707079.html.

42. *Mission-Shaped Church*, 40.

43. Petersen, *Church without Walls*, 111.

44. Murray, "Christendom and Post-Christendom," 5.

45. Miroslav Volf, "Soft Difference: Theological Reflections on the Relation Between Church and Culture in 1 Peter," *Ex Auditu* 10 (1994), http://www.yale.edu/faith/downloads/soft-difference-church-culture.pdf.

46. Karen H. Jobes, *1 Peter*, Baker Exegetical Commentary on the New Testament (Grand Rapids, MI: Baker, 2005), 23–41.

47. Ibid., 38.

48. Ibid., 62.

49. Volf, "Soft Difference."

50. J. Ramsey Michaels, *1 Peter*, Word Biblical Commentary (Waco, TX: Word, 1988), *xlvi–xlix*.

51. Jobes, *1 Peter*, 1.

52. I. Howard Marshall, *1 Peter*, IVP New Testament Commentary Series (Downers Grove, IL: InterVarsity, 1991), 14.

53. P. J. Achtemeier, *1 Peter*, Hermeneia (Minneapolis: Fortress, 1996), 174.

Chapter 2: Everyday Community

1. See Randy Newman, *Questioning Evangelism: Engaging People's Hearts the Way Jesus Did* (Grand Rapids, MI: Kregel, 2004), 55.

2. Stuart Murray, *Post-Christendom: Church and Mission in a Strange New World* (Carlisle: Paternoster, 2004), 1.

3. Timothy Keller, "Late Modern or Post-modern?" *Redeemer City to City*, October 4, 2010, http://redeemercitytocity.com/blog/view.jsp?Blog_param=214.

4. See *Chronological Bible Storying*, http://www.chronologicalbiblestorying.com.

5. See *Echo: Discover the Art of Bible Storying*, http://www.echothestory.com.

6. Miroslav Volf, "Soft Difference: Theological Reflections on the Relation Between Church and Culture in 1 Peter," *Ex Auditu* 10 (1994), http://www.yale.edu/faith/downloads/soft-difference-church-culture.pdf.

7. From Timothy Keller, "The Missional Church," June 2001, http://www.redeemer2.com/resources/papers/missional.pdf.

8. "The Crowded House Values," July 2008, http://www.thecrowdedhouse.org.

9. Karen H. Jobes, *1 Peter*, Baker Exegetical Commentary on the New Testament (Grand Rapids, MI: Baker, 2005), 4.

10. Alan J. Roxburgh and M. Scott Boren, *Introducing the Missional Church* (Grand Rapids, MI: Baker, 2009), 79.

11. Lois Barrett, "Missional Witness: The Church as the Apostle to the World," *Missional Church: A Vision for the Sending of the Church in Northern America*, ed. Darrell L. Guder (Grand Rapids, MI: Eerdmans, 1998), 127.

12. Os Guinness, *Prophetic Untimeliness: A Challenge to the Idol of Relevance* (Grand Rapids, MI: Baker, 2003), 15.

13. H. Richard Niebuhr, *Christ and Culture* (New York: Harper & Row, 1951).

14. John Howard Yoder, "How H. Richard Niebuhr Reasoned: A Critique of *Christ and Culture*," in *Authentic Transformation: A New Vision of Christ and Culture*, ed. Glen H. Stassen, D. M. Yeager, and John Howard Yoder (Nashville, TN: Abingdon, 1996), 69.

15. Os Guinness and David Wells, "Global Gospel, Global Era: Christian Discipleship and Mission in the Age of Globalization," The Lausanne Global Conversation, 2010, http://conversation.lausanne.org/en/conversations/detail/10566/.

16. Miroslav Volf, "Soft Difference."

17. Ibid.

18. Jobes, *1 Peter*, 62.

19. Timothy Keller, "What Is God's Global Urban Mission?" The Lausanne Global Conversation, 2010, conversation.lausanne.org/en/conversations/details/10282.

20. See Tim Chester and Steve Timmis, *Total Church* (Nottingham: Inter-Varsity, 2007; Wheaton, IL: Crossway, 2008), chap. 3.

Chapter 3: Everyday Pastoral Care

1. Dietrich Bonhoeffer, *Life Together* and *Psalms: Prayerbook of the Bible* (Minneapolis: Fortress, 2005), 36.

2. Ibid., 37–38.

3. Ibid., 34.

4. From Tim Chester, *You Can Change* (Nottingham: Inter-Varsity, 2008; Wheaton, IL: Crossway, 2010).

Chapter 4: Everyday Mission

1. Nick Spencer and Graham Tomlin, *The Responsive Church: Listening to Our World, Listening to God* (Nottingham: Inter-Varsity, 2005), 113.

2. Thomas R. Schreiner, *1, 2 Peter, Jude*, New American Commentary (Nashville: Broadman, 2003), 139.

3. John Finney, *Finding Faith Today: How Does It Happen?* (London: British and Foreign Bible Society, 1992).

4. Mark Greene, *The Great Divide* (London: London Institute for Contemporary Christianity, 2010), 8.

5. Adapted from Michael Foster, "Missions and Community through the Ordinary," *M. Scott Foster*, September 11, 2008, http://mscottfoster.com/.

6. Jonathan Dodson, "Eight Ways to Easily Be Missional," April 7, 2009, *Church Planting Novice*, http://churchplantingnovice.wordpress.com/2009/04/07/8-ways-to-easily-be-missional.

7. Ibid. Used with permission of the author.

8. G. K. Beale, *The Temple and the Church's Mission: A Biblical Theology of the Dwelling Place of God* (Downers Grove, IL: InterVarsity, 2004), 25.

9. Paul Barnett, *Apocalypse Now and Then* (Sydney: Aquila Press, 1989), 152.

10. Stuart Murray, *Post-Christendom: Church and Mission in a Strange New World* (Carlisle: Paternoster, 2004), 217.

11. George R. Hunsberger, "Mission Vocation: Called and Sent to Represent the Reign of God," in *Missional Church: A Vision for the Sending of the Church in Northern America*, ed. Darrell L. Guder (Grand Rapids, MI: Eerdmans, 1998), 108.

12. Karen H. Jobes, *1 Peter*, Baker Exegetical Commentary on the New Testament (Grand Rapids, MI: Baker, 2005), 204.

13. Hunsberger, "Mission Vocation," 108–9.

14. Spencer and Tomlin, *The Responsive Church*, 99.

15. From Alan Hirsch with Darryn Altclass, *The Forgotten Ways Handbook* (Grand Rapids, MI: Brazos, 2009), 97.

16. Rodney Stark, *The Rise of Christianity: How the Obscure, Marginal Jesus Movement Became the Dominant Religious Force in the Western World in a Few Centuries* (New York: HarperCollins, 1997).

17. Cited in Leonard Verduin and Franklin Hamlin Littell, *The Reformers and Their Stepchildren* (Grand Rapids, MI: Eerdmans, 2000), 28.

18. Ibid., 28.

19. Hirsch, *The Forgotten Ways*, 85.

20. Henry Chadwick, *The Early Church* (London: Penguin, 1976), 56.

21. Michael Aquilina, "A Double Take on Early Christianity: An Interview with Rodney Stark," The National Institute for the Renewal of the Priesthood, July 22, 2004, http://www.jknirp.com/stark.htm.

Chapter 5: Everyday Evangelism

1. Timothy Keller, *The Reason for God: Belief in an Age of Skepticism* (New York: Dutton, 2008), 173.

2. See Nick Pollard, *Evangelical Made Slightly Less Difficult* (Nottingham: Inter-Varsity, 1997), part 1.

3. See Randy Newman, *Questioning Evangelism: Engaging People's Hearts the Way Jesus Did* (Grand Rapids, MI: Kregel, 2004) and Tim Downs, *Finding Common Ground: How to Communicate with Those Outside the Christian Community . . . While We Still Can* (Chicago: Moody, 1999), 128–33.

4. On surface idols and deep idols see Julian Hardyman, *Idols: God's Battle for Our Hearts* (Nottingham: Inter-Varsity, 2010).

Chapter 6: Hope at the Margins

1. Cited in Karen H. Jobes, *1 Peter*, Baker Exegetical Commentary on the New Testament (Grand Rapids, MI: Baker, 2005), 89.

2. Cited in Edmund Clowney, *The Message of 1 Peter*, The Bible Speaks Today (Nottingham: Inter-Varsity, 1999), 145.

3. See Tim Chester, *The Ordinary Hero: Living the Cross and Resurrection* (Nottingham: Inter-Varsity, 2010), 54–55, 122–25.

4. John Calvin, *Institutes of the Christian Religion*, vol. 1, trans. F. L. Battles, ed. J. T. McNeill (Edinburgh: Westminster, 1961), 3.19.9.

5. See further Tim Chester, *The Busy Christian's Guide to Busyness*, 2nd ed. (Nottingham: Inter-Varsity), 2008.

6. Clowney, *The Message of 1 Peter*, 205.

GENERAL INDEX

SCRIPTURE INDEX

SCRIPTURE INDEX

Porterbrook
Network
Theology *for mission*

Porterbrook Learning

- Designed for all Christians who want to become more mission-focussed
- No prior theological education required
- Whole-of-life training with studies in Bible and Doctrine, Character, Church and Engaging with the World
- Flexible study schedule with weekly seminars or distance learning with residentials
- Learning sites and local groups across the UK

'Affordable, high-quality training for mission and ministry in the 21st century. I warmly recommend it.'
Tim Keller, Senior Pastor, Redeemer Presbyterian Church, NY

Porterbrook Seminary

- Bible college-level programme of study
- Integrate theological training with uninterrupted involvement in ministry
- 10-15 hours of study per week
- Course taught through residential weeks, seminar days and guided reading

www.porterbrooknetwork.org
Directors: Tim Chester and Steve Timmis

IS YOUR CHURCH
a total CHURCH?

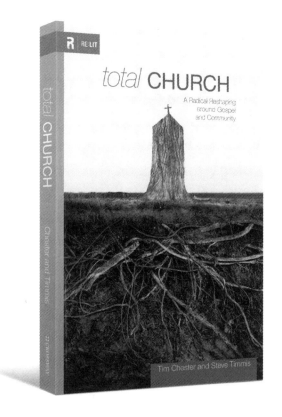

Chester and Timmis emphasize two overarching principles to govern the practice of church and mission:

GOSPEL *and* COMMUNITY

This insightful book calls the body of Christ to apply these standards to evangelism, social involvement, church planting, discipleship, youth ministry, and more, urging the body of Christ to rethink its perspective and way of life.